Passion in theory

GW00994582

'An amazingly elegant and erudite tour through the territory of Freudian and Lacanian psychoanalysis from a self-stated philosophical perspective which transforms the "scene" of psychoanalysis in a quite extraordinary way.'

Moira Gatens, *University of Sydney*

The mind–body problem, or the relation between mind and the material world in general, is one of the oldest philosophical problems. It is also the central question of psychoanalysis as a theory.

All psychology starts from the distinction between the inside and the outside, and psychoanalysis asks *how* that distinction is to be drawn. It seems odd, then, that it is only in Continental philosophy that psychoanalysis has been influential – its marginal status in the Anglo-American tradition, in particular in the philosophy of mind, must seem surprising.

Passion in Theory explores the philosophical possibilities of psychoanalysis, focusing on the 'metapsychological' theories of Freud and Lacan. Robyn Ferrell argues that psychoanalysis, and the concept of the unconscious in particular, offer philosophy important theoretical opportunities. It is an argument that students, teachers and professionals in psychoanalysis and philosophy cannot afford to ignore.

Robyn Ferrell is Lecturer in Philosophy at Macquarie University, Australia.

Warwick Studies in European Philosophy
Edited by Andrew Benjamin
Senior Lecturer in Philosophy, University of Warwick

This series presents the best and most original work being done within the European philosophical tradition. The books included in the series seek not merely to reflect what is taking place within European philosophy, rather they will contribute to the growth and development of that plural tradition. Work written in the English language as well as translations into English are to be included, engaging the tradition at all levels – whether by introductions that show the contemporary philosophical force of certain works, or in collections that explore an important thinker or topic, as well as in significant contributions that call for their own critical evaluation.

Passion in theory
Conceptions of Freud and Lacan

Robyn Ferrell

London and New York

First published 1996
by Routledge
11 New Fetter Lane, London EC4P 4EE

Simultaneously published in the USA and Canada
by Routledge
29 West 35th Street, New York, NY 10001

© 1996 Robyn Ferrell

Typeset in Times by
RefineCatch Limited, Bungay, Suffolk
Printed and bound in Great Britain by
Clays Ltd, St Ives plc

British Library Cataloguing in Publication Data
A catalogue record for this book is available from the British Library.

Library of Congress Cataloging in Publication Data
Ferrell, Robyn
    Passion in Theory: Conceptions of Freud and Lacan/Robyn Ferrell.
    p.   cm. – (Warwick studies in European philosophy)
    Includes bibliographical references and index.
    1. Freud, Sigmund, 1856–1939.   2. Lacan, Jacques, 1901–.
    3. Psychoanalysis.   I. Title.   II. Series.
    BF109.F74F46   1996
    150.19′5–dc20   96–11543

ISBN 0–415–09019–9 (hbk)
ISBN 0–415–09020–2 (pbk)

For Dean

Contents

Acknowledgements

I want to thank the many people who helped me in writing this book, including: Andrew Benjamin, Dean Coulter, Ros Diprose, Moira Gatens, Anna Gibbs, Liz Grosz, Teresa de Lauretis, Jenny Lloyd, Jeff Malpas, Cathy Vasseleu and colleagues and students of Macquarie University. An earlier version of Chapter 4 appeared under the title 'The passion of the signifier and the body in theory', in *Hypatia* (Fall 1991).

Introduction

The central problem of a psychology is the relation of the 'inside' to the 'outside'. But this relation is already assumed in the detail of any psychological theory. Psychology begins as a particular problem in philosophy: i.e., what is the nature of the mind, this extraordinary site of philosophy? It is an old and respectable problem – indeed a founding problem for philosophy, and a self-defining one. It is Socrates' directive to 'Know thyself'.

But it currently also arises as a scientific task, since the question of the relation of the inside to the outside raises not just the necessity of self-reflection, but the question of knowledge. This question has for the several centuries of modern philosophy been taken up with empiricism. The basic commitment of empiricism is to knowledge found outside the self; more strictly, to knowledge as derived from that of the outside which impinges on the self, through the senses. The concern of psychology is shifted to the surface of the distinction between this inside and outside, which meets somehow on the verge of consciousness, in the sensory experience; on the body.

It is on this conceptual scene that psychoanalysis opens. But it is always a drama in the mind's eye. The drawing of a distinction between an inside and an outside, between a mind and its body in the first instance, is always made in theory. In practice, consciousness is an inconclusive experience, joined in delirious flux with its seeming others. How can one, for example, conceive of a mind without the body? or of experience as separated from the senses, or from the phenomena which apparently provoke them? Empiricism is in the same position as idealism, phenomenology and other rivals, in being obliged to presuppose a configuration of terms, and in postulating an arrangement of them which its constituency finds plausible. This will necessarily be a philosophical exercise.

The great innovation of psychoanalysis is its rendition of the set of relations between consciousness and its others. The 'discovery' of the unconscious is the new theoretical opportunity offered to consciousness for self-definition, in the wake of science which has separated, in theory, the subject from the object. The unconscious is then that with which consciousness struggles, all that which lies beyond itself, both mental and material. And as theory, psychoanalysis gives itself a place between rationality and its others. As a theoretical endeavour, it emerges itself as a kind of consciousness, its nature being to give itself a place, and to give these others their place.

This book examines that configuration as psychoanalysis has imagined it. First, in considering the theory of Freud, his 'metapsychology', and then in a consequence of it, Lacanian theory, which brings the argument explicitly to what is speculative in the psychological enterprise in general. The book outlines philosophical possibilities in psychoanalysis, and the shape of an evolving set of concepts which gain philosophical purchase and which provide the energy and compass of diverse contemporary moods.

Consciousness begins from that which is present to it. What is the character of the mental? For psychoanalysis, the theoretical task is to understand how ideas can both depict putative states of affairs – propositional, with content, meaning and therefore the possibility of truth – and how they can have materiality, as energies, motions, instances and events. Psychoanalytic theory begins from the 'mind–body problem', out of a scientific necessity to comprehend the material of the mental. For in science, it cannot be sufficient to accept a dualism of spirit and matter; the problem must be investigated in terms of how the mind, and not merely the brain as a physical deputy, could be said to be material. Materialism depends on this being possible.

For Freud, the dream is a case-study, not only of the theoretical innovation of 'the unconscious', but of the mental in general. It can be interpreted, which brings it within reach of the metaphors of reading and rhetoric. Dream interpretation highlights the character of the mental as image, when the dream is seen as prototypic of the mind. But the mental is also shown, by the example of the dream, to be wishful, motivated. Its images are supported by impulses, upheld by desires.

Looking at the problem from the other side, the prototype of the somatic is the instinct for Freud. The instinct is bodily energy that demands satisfaction. That satisfaction is found in the field of the mental, in representation of it. But the actual impulse itself, the energy which supports this system of images cannot be represented as image; it is therefore not a mental item and yet the mental is an inherent part of its process. There is a gratification possible in the representing of image – this can be seen in the dream, which satisfies itself through depiction; there is a satisfaction posited in representing at all. In this way, energy is yoked to image in the character of the mental.

These, then, are the concepts which set the terms of the psycho-analytic perspective: image and impulse, representation and energy, sign and desire. The unconscious is a postulation; it suggests there is something of the mental in which the duality can more clearly be seen. For this analysis, the finished products of consciousness are almost useless; they are too completely refined in the apparent division that produces the 'mind–body' effect. But somewhere, prior to these perceptions, there is better evidence of the ambiguity; there must be mental entities which combine the two characteristics. The 'primary process' thinking does so, for Freud; this is the unconscious.

In the Freudian view, the mind has its responsibilities to the body. In the notion of the mind as an apparatus dedicated to the accomplishment of the body's pleasure, Freud's materialism produces an 'interpretation of life'; a highly speculative edifice. The potency of instinctual energy is imagined to support the whole progress of civilisation, and represents the relation of an individual to society. It is no accident that it is 'libido' – sexual energy – which is co-opted to development, since sexuality is the liminal state between individual and social. It is that function in which the individual embodies the social.

But at the same time, the process by which this energy is harnessed, including the mental apparatus that organises it, is viewed pessimistically by Freud. It is unlikely to result in satisfaction of the individual – in happiness – and for a constitutional reason. The condition of its discomfort is in its own material support. The body is as much a place of pain as it is of pleasure. Further, both pain and pleasure, happiness and unhappiness, are creatures of the body; they are felt.

In this way, the likely satisfaction brought by any love-object will always only be half the story of the instinct. To have 'everything one wants', even were external circumstances so yielding, could not remove from the equation the unpredictable internal scene. Freud depicts this in the conflict of 'life' and 'death' instincts, characterising the seeming endemic misery of the human mental arrangement.

The theory of sexuality, the organising of pleasure and pain in the psychical structure and the harnessing of libido to social ends, traces a history of events in each individual. As a result, sexual proclivity is by no means the only feature outlined; a person's very character takes shape under the influence of this history. Now Freud outlines in detail what his abstraction of the relation of mind to body amounts to. As a 'geology', the individual is a formation of many structures, weathered and shaped by its 'environmental agents'. Perhaps the crucial formation given the individual is that of gender, with its far-reaching consequences for the conduct of life. The analysis of heterosexuality as a complicated subordination of individual desires to collective ends leaves open the possibility of its contingency and even its failure.

In the concept of the transference, the analysis is pursued from another angle. The passage of libido is experienced in the present, in its capacity to make experience. The perspective suggests a strange plasticity in occurrence and event. The analyst in practice becomes a technician of experience. As a theoretical conception, the transference outlines the construction, not merely of subjectivity, but of the social reality prefigured in the idea of an appropriation of individual instinctual energy by civilisation. That each of us might bring about our fate – Freud's 'fate neurosis' – is only a more poetic rendering of the theoretical project, to depict the human organism meeting its instinctual dictates.

Taking stock of the theoretical project of psychoanalysis at the end of a reading of Freud: what stands out is the continuing effort to conceive of a certain predicament of the mind, to locate it and describe its location consistent with certain empirical effects. The priorities are unmistakably materialist – the mind is embodied, and is not experienced otherwise; the body while distinct from the environment in its specific needs and capacities is never autonomous of it, and indeed cannot survive without its relation to it. The mind inherits this position as its task.

In reflecting on what consciousness must be, Freud concludes it is nothing other than the event of representing – of joining the image of a thing with a word for it – and doing so as an act of perceiving. On Freud's account, scientific theory, too, makes its objects visible by such perceptual acts. And, since every science is a 'figurative language', this is always in the medium of the sign. The satisfaction of giving theoretical form to these intuitions is not unlike the satisfaction Freud supposes there to be in bringing things to consciousness in general. In perceiving scientific effort as one more intellectual response to the environment and the task, Freud reflects on theoretical procedure as itself a kind of representation.

The term 'metapsychology' is the one he gives to the process of postulating structures which are implied by the empirical (that is, the psychological) data. The capacity of Freud's metapsychology to broach questions of its own activity reflectively – its natural inclination to do so

– makes explicable its theoretical passage to philosophies which on their surface are very unlike Freud's own scientific style. In particular, it allows Lacan a kind of theoretical self-consciousness from which he can claim his theory as a 'return to Freud'. The structural affinities between them belie the apparent difference.

Lacan takes up the problem of the relation of the inside to the outside, and begins his elaboration of Freud, through the metaphor of the virtual. The mind is visualised as a surface of apparent depth – the mirror. Knowledge is now a reflection of an external object for an inner gaze. Love becomes a self-reflective gaze, for in the mirror I see myself. But the mirror marks all images of its objects with narcissism, and hence, as paranoic; Lacan conceives of knowledge, no less than love, as having a 'paranoic structure'. In this metaphor of the virtual, he focuses as much on the uncanny features of the mirror as on its faithful habit of reflection.

The images of the dream were for Freud 're-presented' to the mind from remembered perceptions; the 'mirror-image' is now recognised in Lacan as a representation and therefore as a sign, according to the tenets of structuralist linguistics – the priorities of social science are here imported into medicine. Lacan describes the psychological subject as a collection of potential signs, and his experience as a structure of signs. Subjectivity becomes a process of making meaning – the uniting of the word-presentation with the thing-presentation, put forward in Freud as a specific hypothesis, finds extension in Lacan's insistence that the unconscious 'is structured like a language'.

The subject has experience only in making a sign of it; perceiving each moment of the flux of being as a discrete union of 'signifier' with 'signified'. Experience is the bodily pulse of the drive in its itinerary through a world of signs. This creates the possibility that is 'transference'; the drive moves through the virtual space of psychical representations, and these representations are 'pieces' of an outside world, the love-objects and objects of knowledge held by the subject in his mirror-gaze. They are, in effect, 'signifiers', affixed for moments of being to states of internal demand, and they necessarily stand for them as their approximation. They represent an adequation, and remain provisional, for the same reason that, in Freud, the image could not represent that aspect of the instinct which is purely energy or force. This is ontology for Lacan; for so is experience had, perceived by the subject as a relation of mind-image to body-force. 'Being' is the potential of the drives and their mental adoptives, taken together.

If the very nature of subjectivity is seen as functioning as sign and signification, then Freud's mechanics of libido will become symbolic systems. This does not make them any less real, which is to say, any less painful. Gender for Lacan, too, is overbearing. Since it is symbolic, it occurs in the domain of law – which formulation elaborates Freud's intuition that sexuality is not natural.

The superimposition of definition on flux, the regulation of desire by law, produces its own discrepancy – that at least between the somatic flux of drive and the mental image representing it. Lacan interprets this as a structural 'lack' in subjectivity, which amounts to an ontological distress. The pain is only more acute and graphic in the case of neurotic and psychotic illness, but the condition is endemic. Lacan interprets the resort to love, to metaphysics, to sexual relations, and to therapy as responses of the same order. But on his view, not in any of these is the lack resolved; it is only possible to disguise or confront it there.

This makes psychoanalysis as a practice a 'pre-ethical' space, as he conceives of it, one where the subject is persuaded to encounter his objects purely in their subjective meaning – what they mean to him in terms of what he demands of them. But the wider world is an ethical space, since it is where one must attempt a relation between *two* terms, self and other, and where the object has a 'life of its own'. The psychological distinction between an 'inside' and an 'outside' to which the argument has been directed, is now refined in a picture of our existential relations of subject to objects, self to others.

If, by Freud, psychosis is 'a disturbance of the libidinal relation to reality', it becomes extended in Lacan to become both an epistemological threat and an ethical obstruction. It is also commonplace. Where Freud speaks of religion as a 'mass psychosis', Lacan will include other licensed collective 'projections' of wishfulfilment, including some scientific and philosophical tendencies, not to mention romantic love, technology and the hope of cure.

The Freud and Lacan offered here are readings in hindsight – perhaps their theoretical influence on certain contemporary approaches will be evident even from this summary. The chapters which follow elaborate how, out of scientific terms and models coined to meet an imaginative scene – that of the place of consciousness in its own scheme – general philosophical positions emerge on epistemology, ontology and ethics.

1 Body

Let us imagine ourselves in the situation of an almost entirely helpless living organism, as yet unorientated in the world, which is receiv-
ing stimuli in its nervous substance. This organism will very soon be
in a position to make a first distinction and a first orientation. On the
one hand, it will be aware of stimuli which can be avoided by muscular action (flight); these it ascribes to an external world. On the other
hand, it will also be aware of stimuli against which such action is of
no avail and whose character of constant pressure persists in spite
of it; these stimuli are the signs of an internal world, the evidence of
instinctual needs. The perceptual substance of the living organism
will thus have found in the efficacy of its muscular activity a basis for
distinguishing between an 'outside' and an 'inside'.

(Freud, 1915, 119)

Freud proposes an audacious thought experiment in the philosophy of
mind. Rather than beginning from the formed mind of the adult, he
invites us to return to the case of the infant, and consider its plight. This
is imagined as a miserable one: unoriented, entirely helpless, over-
whelmed with sensation and obliged to respond in some way compat-
ible with survival. What Freud then describes is what could be called a
proto-intellectual activity; the 'basis for a distinction' is found, between
'an outside and an inside'.

It is a decisive moment for his psychology. The 'outside' and the
'inside' portrayed in this thought experiment are positioned around the
body, not the mind. The basis of this distinction is a curious one; for a
conventional philosophical understanding of the distinction, it is the
'inside' that represents the known place and the 'outside' that presents
the danger. But on Freud's account, the 'inside' presents the anxiety,
because one cannot avoid the pressure of its need. That pressure is the
germ of Freud's notion of the instinct.

The distinction is made on the basis of the body, in terms of what can be avoided through the nervous system, by initiating action – withdrawing a limb, for example. This cannot be effective in terms of the instinctual need because its demands are more complicated. They require satisfaction, or something like it. This thought experiment reveals at the outset the Freudian commitment to *want* as a basic category in human being. The dependent predicament of the infant reveals that it is not perception that could be said to be its first problem, but need. And the idea of the exigency arising from need provides the prompt for later development.

What happens at the 'surface' of that distinction, at the interface, is the mind.[1] On Freud's account, the mind is an elaboration or a development consequent upon the demand of the body for some response to its need. The mind, to that extent, can be seen as an elaboration on the somatic predicament, and it represents an evolutionary adaptation made by the species to its material condition of vulnerability.[2]

But, 'there is naturally nothing to prevent our supposing that the instincts themselves are, at least in part, precipitates of the effects of external stimulation, which in the course of phylogenesis have brought about modifications in the living substance' (Freud, 1915, 120). What does the notion of phylogenesis serve to depict? An archaic relatedness between organism and environment, a permeability of 'inside' and 'outside', which becomes explicit in the story of life and death told in 'Beyond the pleasure principle'. The narrative appears here in condensation: 'On the one view, the individual is the principal thing, sexuality is one of its activities and sexual satisfaction one of its needs; while on the other view the individual is a temporary and transient appendage to the quasi-immortal germ-plasm, which is entrusted to him by the process of generation' (1915, 125).

Philosophy has tended to approach the situation from the other direction, seeing the sovereignty of the mind over the body. But once the problem is characterised in this way, it creates a complication immediately for the classical distinction. It produces *three* terms: body, mind and world. This 'something' which has been interposed as an interface spoils philosophical expectations.

It places the mind in an awkward philosophical position, being indebted to two 'outsides'. There is the external world, which it must respond to through the senses, but there is also the body, whose pressure demands a response. In this way, the three-part conception overturns the traditional mind–body distinction.

If we now apply ourselves to considering mental life from a *biological* point of view, an 'instinct' appears to us as a concept on the frontier between the mental and the somatic, as the psychical representative of the stimuli originating from within the organism, and reaching the mind, as a measure of the demand made upon the mind for work in consequence of its connection with the body.

(1915, 121)

The definition raises some alternative possibilities for the distinction of mind and body. In explaining mental life from within biology, the instinct is seen not just as a bodily parallel in the mind, but as an intrusion into it, a pressure brought to bear on the mental. Although the mind is in itself the elaboration of the somatic, the distinction between mind and body is not completely effective.

The instinct is a threshold concept – more than a stimulus, Freud is happy to say, the instinct is a 'need' and what it needs is 'satisfaction'. Freud, further subordinating the mind to the body, notes that this representative is 'the measure of the demand made on the mind for work in consequence of its connection with the body'. So its author is the body and its master or employer can be seen to be the body. *Ideas are performed in the service of the body.* The mind is in the service of the body, and the instinct is the go-between, the threshold concept, energetic in some aspects and representational in others.

The instinct is registered on the frontier; the pressure, the need, is felt by the creature as requiring a response. In that sense, the instinct has a somatic character. But *in psychology* it is seen as the psychical representative of that pressure, which can only be as a representation, an idea or something mental. This first distinction is made not on the basis of observation, but on the basis of feeling.

Another way of characterising this 'demand for work' is to imagine the instinct as that need which requires a mental process as part of its satisfaction – which is, one could say, directed through the mental. Since the instinct is on the threshold, belonging as much to the mind as to the body, it is not a mere echo in the mind of the body but depends on its appearances in the mind for its satisfaction. This is why, when Freud breaks up the instinct into its parts, we see that at least one, 'the object', is inherently an image, and that the satisfaction of the need must include this image.

The body on this view is now as threatening to the mind as the external world, with its many dangers and stimuli, even though it is to the body that the mind owes its existence – and the need for its existence. To say the mind is representative suggests a double meaning, a political metaphor.[3] As the deputy of bodily needs, the mind is the body's agent. The mind develops a structure capable of gaining some satisfaction of those needs, but this is such a complex procedure that profound conflict paradoxically arises between the needs of certain instincts and the need of the structure to protect itself. Where a need is not capable of satisfaction without this cost (a 'loss of self', in effect) then repression becomes the mind's defence of itself against the instinct's constant demand. Freud's metaphor draws on political wisdom that preservation of the institution takes precedence over any specific instance of satisfaction of its constituency's demand.[4]

Because the first distinction between 'inside' and 'outside' does not emerge as a straightforward opposition, the mind develops complex and even duplicitous techniques for negotiation. Philosophically, this produces a conception of mental life that is not a mere registry of impressions of the external world, but is instead a kind of poise between an internal pressure and an external exigency. The mind is a field of negotiation, between two intransigent forces, the need for survival and an indifferent world. Psychical development, from this 'helpless organism' to the philosopher-king, becomes a history of the negotiation of that contest. This negotiation entails increasingly sophisticated and elaborate structures at that interface, which in turn, increasingly rigid, becomes the edifice we know as character.[5] Its foundation, however, is always the pressure of instinct, and it is upheld by want. For Freud, there are some things the organism wants for, of which it stands in need by its nature, and the satisfaction of these lies outside it in some important respect. Even in the simple needs of hunger and thirst, something of the 'outside' must be brought 'inside' – the distinction was never secure. This places desire at the centre of an account of personal identity, and it places the body there, too, and the capacity of the body to satisfy its desires.[6]

In examining the instinct as it is met with in psychical life, Freud identifies three instinctual components germane to its representational aspect – *pressure*, *aim* and *object*. The fourth, the *source*, remains opaque because it is somatic – it is that which is not represented psychically, or better, is that which *is rendered by* the psychical representation. This is why it is so difficult to decide how many instincts there are, and what their function is. Because they are truly somatic, they lie in the body and are only known by their psychical representatives. A translation is immediately effected of a somatic state of affairs, deduced from representations given at the psychical level. To sense the instinct is to feel through a material the shape of something underneath.[7]

This is why Freud appears comfortable with the fragmented state of his theory of the instinct – noting, for example, the obscurity of the death instinct as against the sexual instincts – and seems reconciled to the partial nature of his account. For he cannot require of himself an account of this 'source' from the point of view of psychology. That account belongs to biochemistry and neurophysiology. What he can observe – almost allegorically – are the psychical representations which the instinct produces in its attempts at satisfaction. Psychoanalysis observes these mostly through the aim and the object. The pressure is the amount of force, the somatic intrusion, seen as urgency of affect – through the pressure, the object and the aim, the instinct is manifested, and comes to be known in analysis. It is through identifying its object and its aim that most is learned about the instinct.

The aim is straightforward: in every instance, satisfaction. The aim is to remove that state of stimulation at its source. But each instinct has its aim, peculiar to its origin in the body. For example, the stimulation of the oral membrane cannot be addressed through another part of the body. Whereas the source and the aim emanate from the body, the object is that part of the world which is annexed to the satisfaction of the instinct, as a representation. 'It is what is most variable about an instinct and is not originally connected with it, but becomes assigned to it only in consequence of being peculiarly fitted to make satisfaction possible' (1915, 122). In the development of sexuality, the aims are modified as the body grows, developing new capacities and subordinating old ones. It is the fact that the aim of the instinct can be deflected that allows for the cultural achievement of sublimation; if it were not possible to dissociate the instinct and to substitute another kind of satisfaction, it would not be possible to perform the operation that the Oedipus complex postulates.

The flexibility of the instinct in the notion of the aim and the object, is what gives it its 'narrative potential'. This is what takes the Freudian concept out of the immutable circuit of the biological 'instinct' and gives it its social/historical character. In response to the bodily need, the process of satisfaction of the instinct entails an elaborate psychical passage. One could also say that the instinct, as much as it is on the frontier of the somatic and the mental, also makes a passage through that frontier, which it carves out. It leads to the inevitable conclusion of the metaphor: the representing of the mental as a record of that passage, i.e. as a kind of text.

Nothing in this account suggests that the source and pressure of the instinct are themselves fixed or given; little indeed encourages us that there is any such 'thing' as an instinct. Freud notes without defensiveness that the instinct is obscure, since it is not accessible from the point of view of psychology. However, he makes this important assumption about the source, that it is an excitation of only one kind of bodily energy. The difference between instincts would not be one of quality, then, for there is no data from which to differentiate, he argues. The distinction Freud draws between two classes of primal instincts – in this paper, between the ego/self-preservative and the sexual instincts – is based on their apparent aim, not on their source. This is the only distinction that psychology could properly observe.

In this distinction, life is represented as a kind of tension and an inherent contest within the subject, between its own individual state and its membership of a species. (The narrative is continued in the programme of Oedipus, because from another perspective, it is the riddle of the Sphinx that presents the subject with the problem of reproduction, asking the question whether in reproducing oneself one is extending the self or creating competition for it.) The theory of the instincts goes itself through some vicissitudes around the distinguishing of these two classes. The development of a notion of primary narcissism reconciles the first tension, between ego- and self-preservative instincts, by allowing that it is our ego which is our first love.[8] The concept of love, with its necessary intersubjectivity, is then analysed in the concept of the transference.

But when the dualism re-emerges in the sequel to this present paper – in, that is, 'Beyond the pleasure principle' – the competition between ego and object has become a postulation of opposing 'life' and 'death' instincts. In the intellectual labour of this later book, the problem of individuation is surrendered to a more impersonal tension.[9]

The discussion of the instinct is 'metapsychological', in that it sets up the terms in which its material might be discussed. Freud gives theoretical expression to observation that is essentially indirect, known not as somatic occurrences, nor even by report from consciousness, but only through a study of unconscious material. But while psychoanalysis may observe instinctual satisfaction only through its changing objects and aims, these are more than a pantomime of a 'real' causal drama going on beneath the skin. In Freud's theory, *something in the idea itself and its meaning are physically pleasurable.*

For example, for the foot fetishist, the images of the fetish object relate to the world of experience; 'the choice of a fetish is an after-effect of some sexual impression, received as a rule in early childhood' (1905, 154), specifically as 'a substitute for the woman's (the mother's) penis that the little boy once believed in and . . . does not want to give up' (1927, 152). This image, of the fetish-object, is not the psychical 'effect' of a chemical process; that would be to portray the fetishist's mental life as a mime. Instead, psychoanalyis sees that his history has intervened in his mind/body at that point, contributing a node of meaning which plays a causal role in the satisfaction of the instinct.

In fact, despite its apparent loyalty to the physical sciences, Freud's theory of the instinct denies that the biological, chemical or neurophysiological is the appropriate mode of explanation for the development of the instinct. In attaching the concepts of 'object' and 'aim' to the somatic aspects of the instinct, he is demanding a theatre in which images and ideas have effects, that is, in which *they are causally operative*. On such a view, the neurophysiological is not more real than the psychological. (The material of analysis is just that; material.) Wittgenstein, in his critique of Freud, denies that the idea can be a cause in this way, describing Freud's theory as 'a muddle between a reason and a cause'. But psychoanalytic theory presents a challenge to this distinction of reason from cause, which is a version of the mental–physical distinction as such. While Wittgenstein (for his own philosophical reasons) asserts that the opposition in Freud is an error, Freud himself traverses it as apostasy.[10]

In defining the instinct as a *concept* on the frontier between the mental and the somatic – which is to say a frontier in our theoretical ordering, and not necessarily in the material it describes – Freud takes on the distinction between mind and body *as a distinction*, and does not assume that mind and body are separate 'in fact'. That the instinct could be seen to be, at one and the same time, both an image and a force makes that plain.

In respecting the distinction between mind and body, the source of the instinct will be found outside the mental, in a somatic state of affairs. The object, on the other hand, could be said to lie conceptually wholly within the mental, since even while it may correlate to some 'thing' in the world (or in the body) it designates a representation of that in a mental image. The aim, too, is an idea – 'being looked at', or 'penetrating' represent a state of affairs. It is the concept of pressure that is the true hybrid, for it is known mentally as urge or desire, but its force is somatic. The urge is a mental item, but it is also felt. If the mind is a place of representations then it is also a place of intensities, of which instinctual pressures are arguably the constituents.

From this we see the theoretical difficulty of representing this conceptual frontier, between the mental and the somatic. Their difference amounts to a conflict between the *metaphors* of energy and image. As a concept, Freud's instinct is a cipher, an empty vessel or placeholder. A concept posited as on the frontier of any distinction is necessarily incoherent.

As a result, Freud's 'instinct' marks the spot of a difficulty, which is no less than the problem that psychoanalysis has set itself in general (in the first instance, when it began with the psychology of hysteria). *Psychoanalysis itself is on a discursive frontier*, attempting an account of the psychical which observes its structural embodiment, despite the distinction of one from the other.[11]

'Modes of defence' develop as an attempt to handle the instinctual demand. The vicissitudes of the instinct are therefore devices for organising energy, but they are also styles of thinking; they are examples of Freud's 'primary process'.

'[T]he essential feature in the vicissitudes undergone by instincts lies in the subjection of the instinctual impulses to the influences of the three great polarities that dominate mental life' (1915, 140). The polarities describe axes along which the instincts must be organised for human psychological well-being; they set the terms of the mind's negotiation of instinctual need.

What Freud calls the 'real', the polarity between the ego and the external world, becomes the subject's comprehension of its 'place in things' – failure, we might hazard, is psychosis. The 'economic', the negotiation of pleasure and unpleasure, describes the subject's relation to itself, expressed as feeling and threatened by depression and disaffection. And the third axis, which Freud calls the 'biological', refers to the poles of activity and passivity which become the masculine and the feminine, on the theory. While this term seems to refer to the 'biological destiny' of the species, this polarity is played out in actuality in the social sphere, and sexual dysfunction is its price.[12]

The very idea of a vicissitude illustrates the concept of an instinct in its Freudian peculiarity. It relates to the notion of unbound energy from the 'Project for a scientific psychology', and illustrates that the instinct is conceived of primarily as a force which can be channelled, harnessed and redirected. It also shows Freud's apparatus in action: the mind, with its capacity for image and representation, develops to answer the continual pressure of instinctual need. But while this pressure is constant, the environment brings satisfaction only sporadically – satisfaction is not a simple matter.

In organising instinctual impulse toward satisfaction, the mind utilises certain properties of representations; the vicissitudes become rhetorical operations. For example, a vicissitude of aim, the 'reversal into its opposite', can only be performed on a proposition, since things do not have opposites in nature. Similarly, the 'turning round upon the subject's own self', which is a vicissitude of object, suggests a grammatical relation; subject becomes object. The influence of rhetoric can be seen in the example he offers of instinctual vicissitude, the sexual perversion of scopophilia/exhibitionism; the satisfaction of this necessarily unites pleasure and idea, since the bodily pleasure is in an image, the 'looking-at' or 'being-looked-at'.

In 'repression', the manner is closer to refusing representation to a demand, i.e. to gagging it. Freud postulates that it is in being refused expression that the unconscious idea is held back from consciousness – or, more precisely, that making conscious is the connection of the 'word-presentation' with the 'thing-presentation' (1915, 201). In sublimation, it is as though the instinctual demand is rendered 'in translation', that is, put into a new form through which it can be satisfied.

The vicissitude of repression occupies a position of conceptual importance belied by the discussion of the vicissitudes in the metapsychological paper of that title. The first two vicissitudes are elsewhere presented as archaic and inferior intellectual operations, which are superseded in mental life by the development of the technique of repression. Even sublimation is not the equal of repression in conceptual importance, even though it is presented as a further advance in mental life and the product of maturity. But, seen as an account of history and development, Freud seems to regard sublimation as only possible following the secure division of the mind at the primal repression, which creates the distinction between conscious and unconscious. From this point, a 'reservoir' of libido is imagined which can be directed into aims beyond the sexual.

If the vicissitudes are viewed as intellectual procedures, the first two can be said to represent the (con)fusion of the subject with its representations. They display a striking mobility in identity between the self and its objects. Freud may reflect a typical anthropological prejudice in characterising this as a more primitive style of thought; these vicissitudes apppear to Freud as superstitious, characteristic also of children. But as features of unconscious thought, of the primary process, they also presumably underlie all our other thinking.[13] These 'primary process' methods of associating images may be seen as less definitive, more ambivalent – they deal less discretely with the various parts of the world. Moving easily from something to its opposite, for example, is characteristic of dream-logic and other manifestations of the unconscious.

Onto a fluidity of association, repression imposes a dramatic restraint. *'I am not the same thing as my images.'* Repression may be seen as *the process of distinction*, looked at as a proto-intellectual operation. It is not too much to say that, in the primal repression, it is consciousness, more than the unconscious, which is distinguished. Repression can be seen as the process of distinction as such – the production of definition. To make a clear uncomplicated distinction, to observe the law of the excluded middle, is seen as a higher order of intellectual operation. But the persistence in its after-image of pathology, 'the repressed', indicates the cost of such a procedure. Something is excluded by definition – the A has a not-A.

If repression is seen as the intellectual operation of distinction, then it permits rationality, overcoming magical thinking and making science possible. This might be seen as progress (and in places in Freud, it is seen as such). But later in life, Freud is less sure; in 'Civilization and its discontents', he suggests that too much satisfaction may be lost in the process, at least as the current bargain is struck between instinctual satisfaction and civilised life.

While the idea of a distinction implies an exclusion, deconstruction suggests what has been lost in that process. If, using this argument, early societies are read as more intellectually 'primitive', then the conclusion is reached that mythology is a less rational – and therefore serviceable – way of viewing reality. But in the light of Freud's comments about the high cost of repression, psychically and somatically, it is not clear that the evolution of reason in the way described is unproblematically adaptive. On one view of the implications of Freud, it might be that the more exact distinction produces the more intense neurosis; and, at the level of culture, that this includes an intensification of the death drive seen in the phenomena of technology.[14]

The Freudian instinct cannot be reduced to a native satisfaction, to anything preordained or given. On the contrary, it is highly plastic and constructed. Even in the lower orders of life, it is improbable that the operations animals perform for their survival are produced by instincts deaf to history and environment in the way the crude distinction proposes. In human biology, at least, it is not that the word 'instinct' is inaccurate, but that somehow that word is *prejudicial* to the kind of theoretical outcome that Freud requires – a concept that affirms the organic quality of this entity, without foreclosing on its plasticity.

In discussing the instinct, the question of its translation has become an emblematic difference between certain readings of Freud. The word in German, *Trieb*, can be translated either as 'instinct' or as 'drive', and in the analysis it actually makes something of a difference which word is used. Strachey, the heroic translator of the *Standard Edition* in which

Trieb is translated as instinct throughout, points out in the general introduction to the edition, that 'my choice of this rendering has been attacked in some quarters with considerable but I think mistaken severity' (Freud, 1962–75, xxiv). He remarks that the term almost invariably proposed by the critics as an alternative to the translation is 'drive', but that ' "drive" used in this sense is not an English word, and this translation aims at being a translation into English'. Elsewhere in the introduction he declares his intention to translate Freud as if he were an Englishman of equivalent social position and scientific interests. 'The imaginary model which I have always kept before me is of the writings of some English man of science of wide education, born in the middle of the nineteenth century' (*ibid.*, xix).

No doubt Strachey is an astute social observer, and has identified the word that would be used in that circumstance. But he has also been, he declares, 'bound by the fundamental rule; Freud, the whole of Freud and nothing but Freud'. How accurately he has rendered Freud as English in the choice of that word! 'Instinct' has the connotation of a concept belonging to the biological or the natural order, as opposed to the social or cultural milieu, and this is precisely what the argument is about. However, rendering it as 'instinct' may give the concept a more fixed sense than the theory proposes. The Freudian concept does not fit neatly into either category – either the biological or the social – but offers an interesting nexus between both.

The question of the translation is more than just a matter of detail. The flavour of Anglo-American readings of Freud hint that the word choice might have been decisive, in naming a difference between Anglo-American and French readings. The German word is a mark of theoretical ambiguity and raises the question: is the concept a programme, an insistent one which must be played out in a certain way to fulfil its biological destiny? Or are we going to read it more as the 'drive' suggests, a pressure in which is suggested a looser relation to the vagaries of development? The account occupying this study desires for Freud's concept the latter mobility.[15] The sexual phases of development in Freud's theory, for example, interpreted not as contingent phases in a social history, but as stages of development programmed into biological human being, produce a normative reading of Freud which, in the hands of psychiatric practice, has become oppressive. It must be said, *this reading is not necessarily a misreading*. This is not to suggest a causal relation between the translation and that conservative reading, but rather that the difference in translation is emblematic of it.

However, that there is room for interpretation is a product of the very distinction that *Trieb* straddles, that between social and biological. The use of 'instinct' throughout this discussion in preference to 'drive', has not been made in order to take a side in the dispute so much as to highlight the *theoretical innovation* that Freud's concept attempts.

2 Dreams

The theoretical labour of 'The interpretation of dreams' is not the interpretation of dreams, but the postulation of the unconscious for which the dream is offered as evidence. If interpreting dreams was all that it had accomplished, then Freud's study of dreams would not have the theoretical interest it does. But it is as an argument for the unconscious that the work's impact can be seen, and the dream is its extended case-study.

The unconscious is presented as an entity, in a diagrammatic way; as a place of images. But in the dream rhetoric – and inherent in the logic of the 'primary process' – the unconscious is also presented as an operation. In fact, the book is remarkable for its confluence of three metaphorics. There is that of textual exegesis, in which Freud suggests the notion of reading in referring to the dream interpretation of the ancients (which is also an arcane art, proximate to sorcery). There are the metaphors of catharsis and healing – in the medical setting of the work, but further, in the attention given to the disturbances of spirit, the passions, to pain and in the excursion into the deepest confidences kept in the dream. And there are the metaphors of hydraulics: industrial metaphors of process, production, mechanism and apparatus – all the romances of nineteenth-century science.

The dream can be called a symptom of the unconscious. The neurotic's dream comes from the same psychical source as the symptom, according to Freud, and the interpretation of the dream throws light on the task of interpreting the symptom (the work of analysis). The symptom is more condensed, and thus more cryptic – dreams then can become a key or a set of clues to it. The symptom, as somatic pain, anxiety or aversion, is more 'laconic' than the images of a dream, and yet it transpires that one can interpret the symptom in the same way as the dream. And this is because they are both representations of the unconscious.

The conspiracy of an 'unconscious' is already written into the idea of a symptom, in the manifesting of an underlying cause. A symptom is *symptomatic*, and to that extent represents something else. The logic of repression and occlusion which psychoanalysis exploits extensively can be seen to pre-exist it in the medicinal sign of the symptom, in which are foreshadowed Freud's relating of pain to function, mystery to explanation, and cause to effect.

Freud postulates that there are two texts needed in order to interpret the dream. One is the manifest content and the other is the latent content, otherwise called the 'dream-content' and the 'dream-thoughts'. Attempts to interpret dreams from the manifest content fail. It is necessary to translate the manifest content into its second text, the dream-thoughts of which it is a transcription, before attempting to give it meaning. One must read the dream according to its separate images: Freud explicitly likens the dream to a rebus, not a picture. It can be broken down into its various images, and the associations with each of these explored. In this way, far from seeming nonsensical, the dream becomes something that is full of meaning.

What is this latent text? The dream-thoughts are a series of thoughts connected with the image, and which can be recovered by undirected association on the part of the dreamer. This 'free association' is unguided and uncensored, and recovers the chain of thoughts that led to the formation of the image. In each case, this means that it is an *empirical* activity that is undertaken in relation to a particular psyche in free association. In advance, one cannot say what a dream will be, and in hindsight one cannot say easily what a dream might mean, without either knowing the dreamer well or being the dreamer oneself. The dream text is particular to the experience of the dreamer, unlike other kinds of text where a vocabulary is shared.

The dream can be read; the metaphor of reading enters in the title, in the notion of interpretation. It can be read according to a rhetoric that is advanced in ch. 6. The two major principles that form the dream are 'condensation' and 'displacement'. In condensation, one image stands for several thoughts. The condensation in a dream is great, since one can record the manifest content in half a page but it may take eight pages to spell out the dream-thoughts which underlie it. Through the principle of displacement, certain emotions or ideas can be transferred onto an image not because of their similarity, but because of their proximity (in time, in space or otherwise).[1]

But the outstanding feature of the dream is its cryptic habit. This suggests to Freud that the governing factor in its production is the necessity for disguise. Why do the dream-thoughts disguise themselves? He notes: 'the dream is not made with the intention of being understood' (1900, 341). Who is the author of the dream, what is the psychical agency which is responsible for the dream and why must it be encrypted in the manifest content? He quotes the legal tag, 'He did the deed who gained by it' (1900, 308). Freud's hypothesis is that the dream is produced through a collaboration between the wish to represent (write) and the desire to repress (censor); the resultant text is therefore muddled. The dream-distortion is nevertheless productive for, through it, *something is represented*.

'When the work of interpretation has been completed, we perceive that the dream is the fulfilment of a wish.' Freud draws the momentous conclusion, significant not just for the dream but for the whole theory of the unconscious. All dreams represent wishes; or rather, their motive is a wish and they represent the satisfaction of it. If they appear to be anything else, it is because the dreamer is ambivalent about the satisfaction of the wish (an anxiety dream, for example, punishes at the same time as it expresses the wish).

But this wishful habit is not confined to dreams. Freud outlines the dream's rhetorical habits as, more generally, characteristic of what he calls 'primary process' thinking, a term designating a style of thought particular to the unconscious. For this reason, the place of rhetoric in the psychoanalytic theory of psychical structure and functioning is, from the beginning, assured. As a result of the continuity between dream, symptom and the unconscious, Freud not only links the postulates of psychical disorder to those of normal mental life, but provides a common rhetoric for all three. But how can it, the dream, fulfil a wish? In answering that question, Freud reaches adventurous conclusions about psychical experience generally.

Perhaps in the idea of manifest and latent texts, the concept of the unconscious is already posited. The latent text is the unconscious of the dream, and it is in exactly the same sense as one recovers the latent text from the manifest, that one recovers the unconscious behind conscious thought and action. The dream, therefore, is already in itself one model of the mind – the mind is a set of images that make up a text.

Freud does not imagine a radical difference between waking and sleeping, on this argument – the dream is a style of thought and can represent *thinking itself* for the theory; as the speech of the patient in analysis also does. The dream is a symptom of the unconscious both in that it is postulated as a product of it, and also in that it mimes its very manner. The dream, in its double text, represents the whole predicament of the divided mind and of repression.

'. . . *but we must remember, the dream is not made with the intention of being understood.*' This implies that there could be some other satisfaction to be gained in representing or giving expression to something. Intelligibility to the reader, we could say, is not the point.

But in fact reading is not the point at all; the text metaphor collapses here, when it transpires that the pleasure of the dream is in the release of desire in image, in the production of desire as image. There is something cathartic postulated in the *Gestalt* of the dream which has little to do with the notion of an audience. The dream writes, then, if it does, 'for itself'. But it may turn out that the dream does not *write* – that this analogy is feeble, and that it, rather, is seen to expend itself in its images. Still, something specific to that image allows expenditure, since Freud's reading shows that the dreamwork is no mere collection of random images. The dream, indeed, is highly specific, if obscure, in its meaning.

As an idea, free association relies on there being a mind 'full of history'; its connections are created through a set of experiences, through actual and not hypothetical events.[2] In this sense, Freud is an empiricist, for he does not believe in transcendence.[3] The structures which govern the mind, for Freud, are empirical; they are either chemical, or neurophysiological, electrical or at least historical, even if the material mechanism cannot at present be observed. For Freud somewhere 'in there', *in the body*, the mind has its material base. This is why he can speak so confidently of 'complexes' and the like, undisturbed by their metaphoric expression (even in mythical terms, such as Oedipus); for he is sure to be describing a reality, albeit figuratively.

The dream proves the empiricist's point (and incidentally compromises philosophy) because if there were a uniform rationality as the basis to psychical meaning, then my dream should be explicable to you. But seeing, on the contrary, that its meaning can only be deciphered in the contingency of my mental associations, then it can be seen that understanding and meaning are quite a local affair. In this, too, the dream stands for the mind – for the psychoanalytic model of the mind – portraying its logic not as a given necessity but as a historical reality.

To understand in what sense the dream can have meaning in these circumstances calls for an aesthetic account that can relate meaning to release in a theory of representation. It requires a view in which the structure of a narrative or myth resonates *in its very performance* as a mode of understanding which is irreducibly physical.[4] Something of this order needs to be assumed of the dream, in order to describe, in terms of meaning, the energetic release it seeks through the medium of image. But Freud approaches this not as a problem for aesthetics, but as a materialist's curiosity; and his 'answer', in the apparatus in which psychical energy circulates, is proposed in ch. 7 of 'The interpretation of dreams'.

In proposing the rhetoric of the dream in ch. 6, Freud is drawing out a metaphor of interpretation, but he is also outlining the kind of 'primary process' thinking he posits as native to the mind. The strategies of condensation and displacement have been fruitfully translated into the textual metaphor – the figures 'metonymy' and 'metaphor' by Lacan – and have seminal effects in the theory. But these styles of thought also represent Freud's other preoccupation with mechanism and mental functioning – their likelihood is predicated on the notion of discharge of energy. The 'explanation' for why contiguity, for example, could make itself a part of the meaning of an image is only cogent when it is seen as an expedient governed by this priority of expression. Despite the occurrence of image and so of meaning, the whole aim of the dream procedure is a yield of pleasure. The aesthetic of the dream involves a possible satisfaction, not only in representing a cryptic proposition, but in making it present (as *re-presenting* suggests), in offering it as a *surrogate experience*. This makes the dream compelling – it not only has meaning, it has life.

As a symptom of the unconscious, then, the dream is also symptomatic of the structure of the psyche. The dream must be so, Freud reasons, since everybody dreams. It is a feature of normal mental life, and an explanation of the dream should explain something of mental life in general. The dream allows psychoanalysis to make the link between mental illness and mental health.

At the beginning of ch. 7 of his study, in which Freud outlines what the dream suggests about the structure of the psyche, he offers us a striking dream, revelatory of that structure:

A father had been watching beside his child's sickbed for days and nights on end. After the child had died, he went into the next room to lie down, but left the door open so that he could see from his bedroom into the room in which his child's body was laid out, with tall candles standing round it. An old man had been engaged to keep watch over it, and sat beside the body murmuring prayers. After a few hours' sleep, the father had a dream that *his child was standing beside his bed, caught him by the arm and whispered to him reproachfully: 'Father, don't you see I'm burning?'* He woke up, noticed a bright glare of light from the next room, hurried into it and found the old watchman had dropped off to sleep and that the wrappings and one of the arms of his beloved child's dead body had been burned by a lighted candle that had fallen on them.

(1900, 509)

Something happens in the phenomenal world to provoke this dream. The haunting emotional content can be interpreted easily enough from the surrounding events,

> But having recognised that the dream was a process with a meaning, and that it can be inserted into the chain of the dreamer's psychical experiences, we may still wonder why it was that *a dream occurred at all in such circumstances, when the most rapid possible awakening was called for.* And here we shall observe that this dream, too, contains the fulfilment of a wish. The dead child behaved in the dream like a living one ... For the sake of the fulfiment of this wish, the father prolonged his sleep by one moment. The dream was preferred to a waking reflection, because it was able to show the child as once more alive. If the father had woken up first ... he would have, as it were, shortened his child's life by that moment of time.

(1900, 510, my emphasis)

For Freud to isolate this significance in the dream illustrates his interest in the 'inner' experience, as opposed to the outer phenomena which usually catch the attention of those describing the plight of the mind. He proposes that the father's desire for his child was greater than the practical circumstances in the world, and – more significantly still – that the events of the external world were interpreted through a system of wishes in his emotional life. This is carried to the point where it becomes more important to the dreamer to see his son alive than to meet the practical threat of a fire.

The psychical priority, in satisfying that wish, tells Freud something about the structure of the psyche, and explains why this dream has 'a particular claim on our attention' in opening a discussion of it. What distinguishes this dream, and dreams in general, 'so strikingly from waking life' is their wishful character. What kind of apparatus must the psyche be, if it prefers the dreaming reality over the waking in this instance? And further, how is it that the dream satisfies the wish? Freud imagines the apparatus as shown in Figure 1. Sense perception enters at left and is registered as a 'mnemic trace' before crossing into the unconscious and, providing it meets no barrier in the censorship, passing into the 'preconscious', where it becomes available to consciousness and can result in motor activity. However, in sleep, the preconscious–conscious system is immobilised:

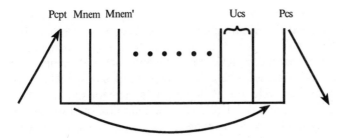

Figure 1 Freud's schematic representation of the psychic apparatus.
Source: Freud, 1900, 541, fig. 3.

The only way in which we can describe what happens in hallucinatory dreams is by saying that the excitation moves in a *backward*
direction. Instead of being transmitted towards the *motor* end of the
apparatus it moves towards the *sensory* end and finally reaches the
perceptual system,

(1900, 542)

producing what Freud will call 'regression' (assuming the natural pro-
gression of psychical energy is toward the discharge of 'motor activity'). The diagram represents the psyche as a system of circulating
energy, in which the wish, as psychical representative of that pressure,
animates the hallucination by reviving the perceptual mnemic trace originally presented to the senses. The characteristic of mental life which
the dream highlights, then, is this: that mental experience on Freud's
view is primarily hallucinatory, and that the representing of mental
items to consciousness, however abstract the idea, must be accomplished by the energetic recourse to the *event* of its perception.

In the ideas of 'primary process' and 'secondary revision', the relation
between conscious and unconscious mentation is sketched. These terms
are not oppositional for Freud, although apparently antagonistic; consciousness arises as exigency in the face of a palpable incoherence: i.e.
the existence of desires which cannot be fully consummated. Lacan
abstracts this to the philosophical nicety that desire by definition is
unrequitable. For Freud, however, the image of contest is a productive
one – consciousness is a kind of sense organ, the ego is a callous formed
at the surface of the mind and as such is more protective than oppressive, and even the mind itself is a mediation between the somatic and its
exterior. These liminal images dominate.

The contents of the dream come under further scrutiny in the function of the 'secondary revision', a kind of rationalising that happens after the event (in all probability, in the memory of it) that also serves the function of disguise. It is itself a strategy of the censorship.

Freud describes secondary revision as the only factor of dream production which is concerned with coherence or rationalising and ordering – he likens it derisively to philosophy and systematic thinking. But this alone of the principles of dream rhetoric reflects a waking concern with comprehensibility, with meaning in its propositional form. The other principles are directed at the aim of representing wishful states as accomplished, in order to experience that satisfaction. The representation in some way allows the discharge of instinctual energy which seeks this pleasure. In other figurations, Freud has represented this as the contest between the reality principle and the pleasure principle, which arises because the mind is the delegate of the instinctual demands to the external circumstances of the environment.

But this makes the reality principle itself an internal phenomenon and one which has its own desire. It is not more 'real' than pleasure, which dictates more frank wishfulfilment. Where secondary revision, or philosophical principle, serves to render the material of experience comprehensible, it can only be by *denying* the origin of its own impulse, the effacement of its own wish.

For example: In discussing the gratification afforded by the 'dream of Irma', Freud notes,

> The whole plea – for the dream was nothing else – reminded one vividly of the defence put forward by the man who was charged by one of his neighbours with having given him back a borrowed kettle in a damaged condition. The defendant asserted first, that he had given it back undamaged; secondly, that the kettle had a hole in it when he borrowed it; and thirdly, that he had never borrowed a kettle from his neighbour at all. So much the better: if only a single one of these three lines of defence were to be accepted as valid, the man would have to be acquitted.
>
> (1900, 119)

This 'kettle-logic' has come to play a part in the use of psychoanalytic reading of wider discourse – Derrida makes use of it, for example, in 'Plato's pharmacy' (in Derrida, 1981). The logic is a fine illustration of the self-serving 'reasoning' of the primary process. While the defendant has no allegiance to truth, his unscrupulous defence is true to his own interests, which dictate he avoid blame.

The kettle-logic describes the curious logic of denial in which rational thought composes itself, gratifying a desire while at the same time repudiating it – indeed, gratifying a desire *by* repudiating it. For the rational includes the wish that it not be wishful; this contradiction obviously cannot respect the law of excluded middle. Thus, the logic is also a defence in the psychoanalytic sense, in terms of being a defence to repressed desire.

But to explain how the disavowal can constitute a gratification requires the concept of the 'censor'. In another register, Freud has described this as one of the more sophisticated of the vicissitudes undergone by the instincts. In effect, he imagines the mental task being the satisfaction of the instinct, i.e. its specific release, which appears in the mind as a wish precisely in order that it can be gratified. But the mind is not in all cases able to grant the wish; yet the instincts are implacable. The mind therefore develops a number of defences against the continuing instinctual pressure. The disavowal is a case of repression which, as Freud describes elsewhere, involves holding the offending idea at a distance from consciousness, from where it must make itself felt in indirect ways. The dream owes its existence to this indirectness, to the tension between distance and satisfaction.

There is a problem with this if one imagines the satisfaction as a *proposition* inherent in the wish. As Wittgenstein notes,[5] it is no fulfilment at all, and even at law (which is strangely faithful to human nature) the part payment of a debt is not regarded as discharging it. But in the energetic economy envisaged by Freud, the idea is always, in a sense, an expedient. As the imagistic representative of a bodily impulse, it can be substituted for by a 'reasonable facsimile thereof'. This 'mobility' is the puzzling hallmark of primary process thinking, and the presupposition necessary to Freud's 'interpreting' dreams at all. It is in the fourth kind of vicissitude, in sublimation, that this mobility of energy/image is most exploited – according to Freud, the Oedipal idea is permanently separated from its energy, which now transfers its weight into a secondary order.

This is reminiscent of Plato's description of philosophy and the classic reflective move declared in the *Symposium*, in which the philosopher moves from the particular instance to the general idea. The psychical development described by Freud is a recasting of a familiar Platonic narrative, of the intellectual and moral progress of the soul. In its allegorical rendition, in the *Phaedrus*, and more schematically in the *Symposium*, the getting of wisdom is seen as a one-way project of enlightenment in which the original sensual pleasure is not lost but is utterly transformed.

The dream satisfies the wish, however partially, by simulating the experience of its satisfaction in the depiction of the circumstances which would imply it. The more opposition the wish meets with from the censor, the more oblique the depiction becomes (and presumably the less satisfying). But since it is not satisfaction at ideational level but release at somatic which is its final court, such dreaming is apparently sufficient to balance the forces animating it.

The rhetorical characteristics of the dream, in deriving from the vicissitudes generally undergone by instinctual energy, have their parallel in all primary process thought. So the symptom too has a wishful character and may condense, displace, reverse and otherwise encrypt the perfectly explicable but repugnant desire. Similarly, in the genre of 'parapraxes', these devices are constitutive. Behind all of it is a notion of proximity, for associations posit no more nor less than actual pathways for the discharge of energy. In whatever realm Freud imagines this actuality to dwell – electrical, chemical or hydraulic – the presupposition of discharge is indispensable to the model.

Further, since this is the foundation for the psyche, these vicissitudes recognised as rhetorical strategies might be expected to underlie all thought. The difference between waking and sleeping is the difference in degree allowed by the contest of the pleasure principle and the reality principle: in waking thought, and especially theoretical thinking, the strategy of secondary revision has a more evident part. So much so, that it transforms itself thoroughly into a simulacrum of an external order. This, however, itself expresses a wish – that for mastery over external circumstance. Surely, in the dream of the burning boy, a place is found for the event in the psychical life of the father because *that dreamed image did satisfy* – however partially, and with whatever pathos, within a situation that human being cannot literally 'master': the advent of death?

The dream of the child raised the hypothesis that the dream satisfies the dreamer by hallucinating an image. In sum, the case of the dream offers two hypotheses:

1 The first is that *the prototypical mental activity would not be perception, but hallucination* (*contra* an empiricism which assumes the primary mental item to be the sense perception). For Freud, hallucination, of which memory is a species, presents the mental in its inevitable character as image.
2 The second is that *the character of the psychical is wishful*, and that it is the wish, not the thought, that is basic to it. This represents the mind's origin in bodily energy and demand.

Freud proposes a psychical reality which is more independent of, and frankly less committed to, external reality than other philosophical accounts. How, then, are we going to distinguish between so-called hallucinations, illusions, mistaken apprehensions of reality, true appearances and so on? But the Freudian model is designed to meet the problem of illusion, since this is a problem involved with the experience of the psychical. In meeting it, it does not 'solve' it – indeed, while the definition of 'psychosis' (which word the Greeks used to describe madness in general) is a 'primary disturbance of the libidinal relation to reality' (Laplanche and Pontalis, 1986, 370), psychoanalysis reveals that it is *the libidinal relation itself* that presents the conundrum.

In pursuing it, Freud displays little interest in the 'thing in itself'. All that is known to mental life are appearances, and, in the case of the dream of the father and son, Freud gives an uncanny prescience of what will be involved in this conviction, since he does not hesitate to accede to the father's portrayal of the real; he 'prolongs the son's life by that moment' of dreaming. This is to understand, in one particular case, what the reality of the dreamer was. Without this sensibility, Freud could not have approached the aspect that made hysteria, as a disorder, so curious: the hysteric suffers from ideas. In general, psychosomatic disorders display a physical expression of psychical conflict, giving the idea a reality in the body. But disorders are always seen as divergences from the normal. The consequences of this attention to psychical reality are more universally illustrated in the case of gender with which psychoanalysis is theoretically preoccupied. In living as a man or as a woman, a reality is created out of a bodily situation, but further, a difference in the material world is dependent on the cultural meaning for experience of it. And this, to the point of despair or satisfaction in unconscious life. How do things become real? Real enough to despair? Pain is the indicator for psychoanalysis. Freud starts out from a domestic reality to which he listens with apparent compassion in the analytic session. But at the same time, trained in positivist science, he appears to accept Kant's distinction between phenomena and noumena and does not record his 'findings' in terms of ontology.

Nevertheless, the Freudian view of the psyche challenges the right of external circumstance, i.e. of an objectivity, to arbitrate in matters between us. It disturbs the assumption that the objective view is a valid – or even a possible – intersubjective reference. This explains the attraction of his thinking for a perspectival philosophy. To the tradition governed by liberal empiricism, and including of course the founding premises of the sciences, this view offers a radical refinement of its 'objectives', by *disqualifying the objective as real;* it makes of the concept of the objective a theoretical innovation and an enabling fiction. In general, because the hallucination does satisfy in some sense, then truth and illusion become second order operations performed on a psychical image. Truth as well as illusion go via the image/hallucination, as their *a priori* – in this, Freud foreshadows a problematic of representation, which he helps to set up.

3   Life

What of the vulgar prejudice, 'Freud makes sex the basis of every-thing'? All apparently comes from the sexual; affection, for example, is represented as 'aim-inhibited' love. Why is Eros insisted on? Freud means to refer to body-pleasure when he uses the word 'libido'. Genital love, a narrower category, is constructed out of many possibilities in bodily pleasure. Freud is a reluctant psychologist – in an insistent sense we remain bodies on the theory; or more accurately, the body is the condition of the mind. Happiness and suffering, pleasure and pain, are firstly *feelings* for Freud, and feeling belongs to the body.

Pleasure is the thing proper to oneself, the characteristic or emblem of the individual. By my pleasure I experience myself. That the mark of the individual should be his or her pleasure grows out of the diagnosis of mental suffering. What is characteristic of me is my pain, says the neurotic. Since I am known in my pain, I am my body not my mind; I feel, I do not see. Even the ego is bodily, as Freud concludes in 'The ego and the id'. And feeling isn't 'mere' body, it also has its 'ideational component', relayed in thought, recoverable in the association of ideas. Depicting the relation between body and mind in Freud seems of neces-sity to go through the notion of the image, as I have argued.

The impressions of the body, of its senses and internal reflections, collaborate in a system of what can only (in terms of the body, whose impressions they are) be further impressions. Impression is meant here in its dual sense: to impress upon, the stamp or contour; and to carry an idea ('it gave me the impression . . .'). This is why the 'thought' is thought on the model of hallucination for Freud: Thought preoccupies the psychoanalyst *as a concrete event in the body*, as a material occasion.

Thought as reason is subordinate; this radical empiricism regards rationality itself as the result of a laborious organic manufacture, and recognises (in the idea of sublimation) that it is taken on lease from the body's energy. Culture and civilisation – including philosophy – emerge as 'reaction-formations' in the vicissitudes of the instincts. Freud is lured into the story about the origins of culture through his attraction to the empirical, to the metaphor of the material event. Grounding his theory in the biological (which is to say the material), in the historical (that is, the event), Freud addresses the question of the adult neurotic's suffering by setting in motion metaphors of history and prehistory; he appeals to childhood and construes sexuality as constructed out of events. It is not surprising that he can find an imperfect analogy for the mind, then, in the ancient city of Rome, since he has already built his conception on the metaphor of history.[1]

Freud starts from the strange fact that we do not seem to remember our own origins:

> Hitherto it has not occurred to us to feel any astonishment at the fact of this amnesia, though we might have had good grounds for doing so. For we learn from other people that during those years, of which at a later date we retain nothing in our memory but a few unintelligible and fragmentary recollections, we reacted in a lively manner to impressions, that we were capable of expressing pain and joy in a human fashion, that we gave evidence of love, jealousy and other passionate feelings.
>
> (1905, 174)

Our lack of incredulity is evidence of a repression, i.e. it is not that we have forgotten our origins but that *we do not remember them*. The determination with which we do not remember betrays the subject as sexual. 'But what are the forces which bring about this repression of the impressions of childhood?', Freud asks.

> It is during this period of total or only partial latency that are built up the mental forces which are later to impede the course of the sexual instinct and, like dams, restrict its flow – disgust, feelings of shame and the claims of aesthetic and moral ideals. One gets an impression from civilized children that the construction of these dams is a product of education, and no doubt education has much to do with it. But in reality this development is organically determined and fixed by heredity, and it can occasionally occur without any help at all from education.
>
> (1905, 177)

Describing the latency period as an '*organic* repression' indicates that the body retains the traces of its history in the individual's stages of development. And yet, the construction of sexuality differs from individual to individual – the theory of the neuroses attests to this. It places this 'organic repression' in an ambiguous light. What indeed is 'organic', as apart from historical, in the life of the mind?

Freud's account of infantile sexuality illustrates theoretical notions developed in 'Instincts and their vicissitudes', where the body as the source of instinctual impulses, grounds the psychical and in fact provokes its development. Freud suggests the self-preservative instincts make the baby not a tabula rasa, but a cry of demand, in the face of the world it has entered. The gratification of that demand takes place in relation to various parts of the body, and those parts are differentiated as highly significant, as psychoanalytic practice reveals. Gratification becomes pleasure, and pleasure is the bribe that Freud portrays Nature as providing to lure us into the game of life – both that of sustaining our own life and of reproducing it.[2]

Freud observes that originally, in infancy, there is a constitutional bisexuality which is merely a subset of a more general disposition he names 'polymorphous perversity'. This is a postulation of receptivity of the organism to the action of history, as experience. The child's body is 'polymorphously perverse', which is to say, capable of experiencing pleasure in various of its parts – pleasure specific to that part. But infant sexuality is *polymorphous*, not amorphous; the child is a set of potentialities specific to its anatomy. The Freudian narrative is shocking in its specificity: how, in relation to the *human* body certain things become eroticised. Within this, nevertheless, there is a plasticity. Life in culture organises the basic anatomy psychically, to produce experience.

The first principle of this view of desires constructed out of polymorphous potentiality is that any bodily function and any bodily need can become the site of erotic aim. Any part of the body which comes into contact with the outside world is changed by it, and this is apart from the changes in one's own body. In 'Instincts and their vicissitudes', Freud describes how the sexual instincts are seen to 'piggyback' initially on the self-preservative instincts, rehearsing the pleasure that was first felt as the satisfaction of need (1915, 126). Freud views the body at the level of sensation, observing that it is possible, through the discrimination of pleasure and pain, to organise an erotics around the events that occur to a body in the course of its life.

The question, 'Why does Freud insist on a sexual basis for everything?', is answered in the theory of sexuality. The culture forms its members, through the medium of their pleasure, into sexual subjects which will reproduce that culture. Seen phylogenetically, civilisation is an evolutionary task, prompted by Eros – the surmounting of embodiment. In 'Three essays on the theory of sexuality', Freud presents this as a plastic involvement of the social environment in the body; the self is posited as interacting with the world and with others, through love. The real tension, on this view, between the individual and society, is in their *proximity*; not their antagonism. They are kin indeed, for the individual is formed in its experience of social life.

But, by 'Civilization and its discontents', Freud considers the social taxes the individual too heavily. As he complains, it rules out the satisfaction of other pleasurable possibilities and disenfranchises the proportion of the population whose inclinations, for reasons of history or 'constitution', are otherwise (1930, 104). This is a serious charge going to the heart of well-being, for the individual, being a body, is nothing other than the capacity for pleasure. The result is pain.

It is the plasticity of the body in its society/environment that makes Freud's theory suggestive beyond the life sciences, for aesthetics and philosophy as much as medicine and psychiatry. Freud's theory leads to the conclusion that bodies differ as their histories differ.[3] Following Freud, we might suppose that under the unparalleled influence of technology on the body – in organ transplant, surgical reconstruction, contraception and genetic engineering – the future body's psychology might differ in inconceivable ways. There is no necessary essentialist nor determinist inflection in Freud's emphasis on the organic and the material.

> Life, as we find it, is too hard for us; it brings us too many pains, disappointments and impossible tasks.
>
> (1930, 75)

Elsewhere in 'Civilization and its discontents', Freud names the project of psychoanalysis as 'our interpretation of life' (1930, 120). At this late stage of its articulation, Freud proposes the theory that began life as a medical procedure, and a style of therapy, to be a rival to the religious system or other metaphysics. Or rather, he proposes it as a successor.

The essay begins from a poet's 'oceanic' feeling, which Freud claims he does not recognise in himself. This is not surprising in one who professes to view religion as an effective painkiller but one which is all the same 'humiliating', as he tells us, since the escape into oneness with the universe is clearly an infantile regression. To the proposal put to him by his poet friend, that the practitioners of yoga have found this state of oneness in altered kinds of consciousness, Freud replies by affirming the light of reason, quoting Schiller: 'Let him rejoice up here in the roseate light!' He asserts the scientific over the religious interpretation of life, the *hydra* of an empiricist-utilitarian-democratic sensibility.

But Freud's work paradoxically brings to light the limit of such an interpretation. He cannot, because of his theoretical object – the mind – and a certain intellectual *courage,* prevent his psychoanalysis from undermining those values. He tells us, in 'Civilization and its discontents', that the theory of the instincts is the most important, but also the hardest, part of the theory – no doubt this arises because the instinct is the concept that addresses the threshold between body and mind.

His imagination, nurtured in the life sciences, naturally pursues this subject within an empiricism, a materialism, but at the same time, it explores the confounding case for the desires of those theories – the mind becomes a scientific object, that of 'the knowing subject'. This is why Freud encounters frustration in regard to the price of civilisation for the individual, the renunciation of instinct. For, in general, the philosophies to which he is apparently indebted – empiricism, liberalism, scientific materialism, utilitarianism – meet their disavowal in the fact of embodiment. Indeed, the great throught-structures that buttress nineteenth-century scientific endeavour exact the very price Freud chides civilisation for asking of the individual: *they deny the body of the knowing subject.* The virtues of those philosophies are turned against themselves, producing a flatness and disappointment – ironically with life – which is exhibited in the style of 'Civilization and its discontents'. But it also produces the energy of its subversion (this is the Freud that appeals to post-structuralism).

The question of the purpose of human life is a question without an answer, as far as Freud is concerned; it is a 'presumptuous' question. But the 'less ambitious' question, of what purpose humans pursue in their lives, is answered by 'the program of the pleasure principle'; they strive for happiness. This is psychoanalysis in a utilitarian frame. The pathos is that this programme and the world are at 'loggerheads': 'There is no possibility at all of it being carried through; all the regulations of the universe run counter to it' (1930, 76). The reasons for this are constitutional, for the intractable feature of our existence is that suffering is endogenous; whatever the cause of our pain, the *place* of it is in the body 'which cannot even do without pain and anxiety as warning signals'. This leads us to the article of his empiricist faith:

> In the last analysis, all suffering is nothing else than sensation, it only exists in so far as we feel it, and we only feel it in consequence of certain ways in which our organism is regulated.

(1930, 78)

Since empiricism was always, to put it in Freudian terms, a 'reaction-formation' against theology and a world of spirits, demons and other transcendentals, the sentiment can be described as an article of faith, for its scientific terms do not disguise its character as an attempt to answer the problem of evil.[4] But in the death instinct, does the mystery of violence intensify the more reason (in the form of science) stares at it? As femininity will, under the weight of masculinity, or the unconscious under pressure of the dominion of consciousness? These symptoms form some of psychoanalysis's fruitful effects.

Suffering is nothing else than sensation, it only exists in so far as we feel it. The shocking plausibility of this sentiment comes from a sense of recognition; we may feel the desire imminent in it. We recognise ourselves in it precisely because the programme of empiricism is the project of our time. *In the last analysis, I am just a body: Take this body from me!* How did we get here, to the wish to be relieved of the body at the same time as, since I am nothing but my body (for what is the soul to a materialist but a humiliating 'palliative'?), *I am reduced to what I feel?* Freud was not always as pessimistic. When he set out on the empiricist's path, his heart was lighter; in the 'Three essays on the theory of sexuality' (1905), we were already nothing other than our bodies, but they were places of pleasure first and foremost, whereas in the 'last analysis', they have been revealed to be places of pain.

The sexual life of civilised man is severely impaired, Freud muses; it sometimes gives the impression of being in the process of involution as a function, just as our teeth and hair seem to be as organs – sometimes one seems to perceive that it is not only the pressure of civilisation but something in the nature of the function itself which denies us full satisfaction (1930, 105). It parallels his growing suspicion that the instincts are not all reducible to sexual ones.

> Since the ego-instincts, too, were libidinal, it seemed for a time inevitable that we should make libido coincide with instinctual energy in general, as C. G. Jung had already advocated earlier. Nevertheless, there still remained in me a kind of conviction, for which I was not as yet able to find reasons, that the instincts could not all be of the same kind.
>
> (1930, 118)

Freud describes the theory of instincts as indispensable to psychoanalytic theory, no doubt because it provides the theoretical bridge between body and mind.[5] But the death instinct emerges as the strange 'unseen hand' in the theory of the instincts, making Freud's body more than a living history of pleasure:

> I can no longer understand how we can have overlooked the ubiquity

of non-erotic aggressivity and destructiveness and can have failed to give it its due place in our interpretation of life.

(1930, 120)

So the belated answer to the 'vulgar' question with which this chapter began: the material of life is not only sex, but sex and death. The recognition of these two great irrationalities in the centre of Freudian theory takes it beyond the liberal theories from which the account grows, of evolution and the triumph of civilised, over instinctual, life.

4 Sex

The account of sexuality that Freud gives is directed at explaining
something that is more often taken as given: how we come by the desires
we have. Freud's theory details an account of the history and structure
of desires, undermining any argument for their self-evidence.

Freud offers a consistent account for the consequences of anatomy *at
the level of the psychical*. He does not rely on explanations like 'chemical', or 'genetic', to solve a problem in psychology, that is, a problem in
his own discourse. He produces a theory that demonstrates at the ideational level the development of sexuality. Although there are the instincts and there is a chemical base to the question of sexuality, on
Freud's view there is neither primordial masculinity and femininity nor
is there a pre-ordained heterosexuality. And while Freud is conscious of
the dictates of species reproduction, which seem to suggest a certain
kind of coupling as generative, even that undertaking is not senti-
mentalised. While accepting the probability that there is a constitutional element in sexuality and in psychical character in general, it is
the history of the individual which is visible to psychoanalysis, and
sexuality is accounted for in these terms.

This means examining the social world in which this organism grows.
It offers an interesting angle on that world, seen as a very material (even
banal) set of circumstances. In the descriptions of childhood given in
the 'Three essays on the theory of sexuality', Freud betrays a domestic
eye and his points are precisely observed, as though he found it easy to
put himself in the position of that child again. The whole of the second
essay on the theory of sexuality is a story about growing up sexually,
and is told from the point of view of the child; this is a real strength in
the account.[1]

Freud's postulation that there is division within the mind, and a
repression of parts of it, suggests that some of our possibilities are not
acceptable to the social persona. That argument starts from the specific

demands the society makes of the individual, in terms of behaviour and attitudes. Murder, for example, is disqualified in the 'anal phase', and incest in the 'Oedipal'. Desires are fashioned in relation to social constraints, which are received by the child as prohibitions imposed by the ones he loves, his parents. The instinct is never destroyed, Freud notes; the mind can only regulate it by deflecting or directing it. This is why the ideas of condensation and displacement become so important, because they are general psychical mechanisms for handling the relation between the instincts and external (including social) demands. This 'instinct energy' becomes sublimated into work and acceptable sexual activity – this Freud describes as an historical process.

The body is a sensual field that is sensitised of necessity as the child is cared for and grows older. Such sensitising in our society is usually carried out in the care of its biological mother, where bodily intimacy can be relied on. The sexual instincts in childhood are auto-erotic, that is, they are without an object. But the demands made from an 'outside' are felt by the baby from the beginning. How they attain the object required of them for 'normal' sexual life is a product of the inhibition and subordination of other tendencies to genital sexuality.

The first glamorous region of the infant's body is the mouth; this is where nourishment is taken in, crucial for survival. The 'oral' is the leading mode of erotic development at a certain time of the infant's life; the child receives satisfaction of the need through sucking and that satisfaction is pleasurable. If it is pleasurable to have need met, it can then be experienced as *pleasure as such*, separate from the consummation of need. This is the point at which the child will deliberately suck the thumb to reproduce the pleasure. The hypothesis is that what was first pleasurable because it satisfied need, now lends itself to auto-eroticism, the child seeking to produce that pleasure for its own sake. Thus, the origins of oral pleasure are archaic – they date from the first experiences of need and satisfaction.

The next leading sensations for the child are anal. In the first place the infant has little control over the muscles which produce micturition and defecation, but as that control becomes a social issue, psychical consequences follow. They becomes themselves a source of erotic satisfaction – as with the oral, the sensation in that sensitive part of the body can effect the same kind of 'transfer' and become a source of independent satisfaction. By the nature of the demand of toilet training, and by other events coincident with it in the infant's life, these become caught up in the register of obedience and submission. In the anal phase, something is demanded of the child and is connected thereby with social place. What happens in the anal phase is a precursor to the Oedipal plot, the learning of complicated lessons on the operation of authority and power.[2]

On Freud's view, the neurotic's sexuality either has not left, or has returned to, the character of infantile sexual activity. But, on closer inspection, we see these characteristics vestigially in all adults. The discussion of the perversions in the first essay shows us the continuum between 'perverse' and 'normal' sexual life, and presents us with our tolerance for perversions (such as kissing) while they remain subordinated to genital sexuality. The fate of thumb-sucking illustrates how Freud understands the sexual foundation of certain adult abstractions:

> these same children when they are grown up will become epicures in kissing, will be inclined to perverse kissing, or, if males, will have a powerful motive for drinking and smoking. If, however, repression ensues, they will feel disgust at food and will produce hysterical vomiting.
>
> (1905, 182)

The infantile sexual instincts, in the ordinary course of things, are adapted through *sublimation* to a cultural end, or come through *reaction-formation* to be part of a person's character. The possibilities of anal eroticism are similarly illustrative:

> The contents of the bowels, which act as a stimulating mass upon a sexually sensitive portion of mucous membrane, behave like forerunners of another organ, which is destined to come into action after the phase of childhood. But they have other important meanings for the infant. They are clearly treated as a part of the infant's own body and represent his first 'gift': by producing them he can express his active compliance with his environment and, by withholding them, his disobedience. From being a 'gift' they later come to acquire the meaning of 'baby' – for babies, according to one of the sexual theories of children, are acquired by eating and are born through the bowels.
>
> (1905, 186)

A profound circuit of associations emerges for the Freudian view; in the prefiguring of the penis and penetration in the faecal mass, and the effort of controlling the bowels required of the child, Freud imagines the question of paternal authority well before the castration complex makes it explicit. Penetration and mastery, gift and exchange, production and reproduction – these lessons in social circuitry are learned on the body. They are extrapolated into one's character in the equation of cleanliness and order, with the normal disgust felt for faeces and, by association, its smell.

Freud goes so far as to imagine the repression of the sense of smell in the evolution of each individual as a repetition of the drama of the civilisation of the species itself. Walking erect, Freud hypothesises, diminished the sense of smell, and prioritised sight; thus provoking sexual desire through the visual and not the olfactory faculty. This will have produced persistent, rather than rhythmic (i.e. according to the menstrual cycle), sexual desire. The consequence of this would be that a man attempted to keep his sexual objects near him (in the tribal setting), and nurturing tasks kept her obliged to him for protection. As a story of the origins of sexual subordination, this is a not-very-interesting corollary to the story of femininity offered in Freud's theory of individual psychology, and suffers from the same defect – that only male desire is considered. But its interest lies in its being an attempt at a phylogenetic account of the matter, which is to say, an attempt to take seriously the body in prehistory, and the history of the body.

> Historians of civilization appear to be at one in assuming that powerful components are acquired for every kind of cultural achievement by this diversion of sexual instinctual forces from sexual aims and their direction to new ones – a process which deserves the name of 'sublimation'.
>
> (1905, 178)

These phases offer examples of the way in which parts of the body take the sensation involved in need, and transmute it into the erotic. But pleasure, erotic pleasure as auto-erotic pleasure, relates specifically to the capacities and the needs of the infant body. Freud postulates that the disorder and the discomfort of that state is a profound motivation to growth and development, since one cannot survive autonomously at that level of disorganisation, and is dependent in an urgent way on the care-giver.

> the exclusive sexual interest felt by men for women is also a problem that needs elucidating and is not a self-evident fact based upon an attraction that is ultimately of a chemical nature.
>
> (1905, 146)

The arguments around Freudian theory, as to whether on the question of sexuality it is liberating or reactionary, usually converge on this detailed account of how patriarchal conjugal heterosexuality is induced to come about in polymorphous-pleasure-loving creatures.[3]

As Freud makes clear in the third section of 'The ego and the id', the renunciation of desire for its first love-object (the mother) is not undertaken easily or willingly by the child (1923, 28–39). It requires the coercion of the castration complex, and thereafter the policing of the super-ego, under whose watchful eye the gratification of desires is regulated.

The social reality that reproduces through heterosexual marriage commands the individual to become part of a structure that guarantees the perpetuation of that reality. The mark of this imperative is the incestual taboo on men, to give up the natural love-object and displace instead onto other like objects. The tragedy of the Oedipus myth, which Freud adroitly appropriates for science, lies in the unwitting nature of the transgression, illustrating that it is not necessary to know the law to be subject to it.

In his theory of sexuality, Freud frees the sexual instinct from its reductive biological givenness and opens it up to social construction. Psychoanalysis as a science, on his conception of it, takes as its scientific object the laws of the unconscious, and should provide explanatory theory of its operations in those terms. It is his rigour, which insists on the possibility of a psychical, or ideational, explanation of psychical development, that lies behind his increasing emphasis on the role of the castration complex in bringing about masculinity and femininity. While always leaving the door open to 'constitution', Freud does not resort to the reduction of this development to the anatomical sex of birth. In this, he is aided by the fact that the anatomical definition of sex is curiously equivocal.

Freud's determination to postulate psychical causes, to be explicated according to the clinical observation of primary thought processes in the unconscious, leads him out onto the scene of culture. But he does not leave biology and anatomy behind; the grounding of the mind in bodily pleasure means that psychoanalysis continually affirms the material nature of that scene. It is exemplified in the significance given to the fear of castration which is dramatised on the body in a literalising of meaning, the biblical 'word made flesh'.

In 'The dissolution of the Oedipus complex', Freud describes the development of infantile sexuality toward its eventual repression. Since this infantile period is ignored and forgotten in the adult world, the anxiety associated with the sexual lessons of this period – and in particular the prohibitions more or less harshly placed on masturbation – are repressed. Nevertheless, Freud concludes that what happens to the individual in traversing the infantile phases is decisive for his or her later health and happiness. In 1924, when that essay was written, the problem of sexual difference was only beginning to present itself. This is parallel with Freud's strengthening conviction of the importance of the castration complex which puts an end to Oedipal wishes. Indeed, it is as a theoretical consequence of this growing emphasis on the psychical importance of the threat of castration that the problem of femininity grows.

Castration is the threatened punishment for masturbation and so for the incestual desire which accompanies it, but the threat is not accepted as credible until the little boy sees the genitals of the girl. Even then, he must struggle with the powerful conflicting demand; the urgent pleasure, the narcissistic fear. Narcissism wins, and the desire is relinquished. The child sees the sexual partner of either object as a rival, and indeed as a successful one. Freud imagines the boy-child performing an inaugural psychical manoeuvre of some sophistication. Whereas frustration has been dealt with before through fantasy or denial, this frustrated demand (i.e. for sexual possession of his love-object) is met by a 'primal repression'. The boy puts aside the demand of the body, in favour of obedience. And there is a bribe offered to the boy, for in learning to substitute, there is promised a substitute – 'another woman like her'. This substitution – the surrender – of the first love-object makes it possible to surrender subsequent objects, and to substitute for them. (Substitution in its full capacity as signification is taken up by Lacan.)[4]

It is not only sexual orientation that is established by the Oedipus complex. Sublimation, too, is the work of its resolution. The greater part of libidinal energy is released for other ends. Having learned to deflect the energy of the instinct, and to substitute for the original love-object, the child is now what they quaintly call 'educable'; it becomes possible to give the child work. Work becomes a second-order erotics, and the beneficiary of these newly directed 'softened' sexual aims. Sublimated bodily energy freed from dedication to sexual satisfaction now permits of other satisfactions.

The super-ego is the internalising of the figure of the father, and the social law, making his an internal voice, not merely an external one. A postulation of self-discipline has emerged. *Now there is something of the outside world in the child's head*; he has reached a psychical compromise with the threat of castration and an agency has been set up to keep the dangerous desire at a distance, and to 'police' it.

As the threat of castration becomes more central to the structural mechanism that makes childhood sexuality into adult sexuality in men, it becomes painfully clear that as a result of an anatomical difference observed between the sexes (his visible genital), the threat cannot work the same way in women. As a solution, the Oedipus complex, and its destruction through the castration complex, gives Freud a structure in each male child's upbringing that can be relied on, under normal circumstances, to bring about a predictable result: the 'manufacture' of men satisfied to reproduce that society by mating in conjugal fidelity and identifying their offspring as their own in name. But his solution presents him with a problem. The more he is able to explain male sexuality, the less he can account for female sexuality.

Freud perceives that castration is an 'accomplished fact' in girls and: 'The fear of castration being thus excluded in the little girl, a powerful motive also drops out ... for the breaking off of the infantile genital organisation' (1924, 178). In 'Some psychical consequences of the anatomical distinction between the sexes', Freud begins to diagnose the problem with the earlier account. He had assumed that the girl's first love was symmetrical with the boy's, and that, as he loves his mother first, so the little girl loves her father. Now he recognises: 'The little girl is a little man'! Children of both sexes love their mothers first, and the Oedipus complex in boys is not the complement of the Oedipus complex in girls. Freud had been misled, then, in the first formulations on femininity by the fable of the two sexes as two halves of a whole, the idea of the sexes complementing each other.[5] Now Freud asserts the girl enters the phallic phase as the boy does, in love with the mother, but once she sees that the clitoris is not as big as the penis, she knows 'in a flash', as Freud (melo)dramatically puts it, that she has been cheated. 'She has seen it and knows that she is without it and wants to have it' (1925, 252). The lack of a penis leaves her with a 'narcissistic wound', the scar of which forms an inferiority complex and the enduring penis envy which is unconscious and gratified in maturity (and then only partially) by the baby as its substitute.

In his account of the castration complex, Freud can be read as identifying the process by which male and female subjects are produced, and the limits and incompleteness of that production. Critical feminist responses to the theory echo targets that Freud himself may have had in mind in drafting the sometimes provocative remarks in the New Introductory Lecture on 'Femininity'.

> Throughout history people have knocked their heads against the riddle of the nature of femininity ... Nor will you have escaped worrying over this problem – those of you who are men; to those of you who are women this will not apply – you are yourselves the problem.
>
> (1933, 113)

Freud indicates that an audience is an audience of men, to which the undeniable presence of women remains an exception.[6] Despite himself, Freud harbours some anxiety about the partial nature of his account: his constant reiteration that 'not much is known', that psychoanalysis cannot give the answer to the riddle of femininity, and his telling defence that the lecture 'brings forward nothing but observed facts almost without any speculative additions' (1933, 113).

In theory, Freud has solved the problem of how both sexes are coerced into giving up their infantile sexual positions in preparation for adult sexuality. The castration complex drives them both out of phallic sexuality – the boy in fear, the girl in disappointment and disgust. But it is ironic that Freud should conclude that the little girl is a little man since what he set out to account for was sexual difference. Irigaray argues the consequence of his account is to reveal the sexual indifference of our culture – that there is but one sex, male, and its negation, which is called female – since it is only in relation to male sexual pleasure, i.e. the pleasure of the penis, that the little girl's development is understood. And in the end it seems that this little man apparently abandons a certain kind of pleasure (that of the clitoris) on the basis of its being 'not-man-enough'. That is, her clitoridal pleasure is not sufficiently like male pleasure to be valued as pleasure, and her desire, in as much as it is feminine, is obscured (Irigaray, 1985).

Freud notes some disparaging 'consequences' for femininity, such as his theoretical suspicion that women are less moral and less just, following from the hypothesis that they do not get as perfect a super-ego.[7] And if one thing seems to be happening for the girl at the time of the Oedipus complex, it is that she grasps that there is not so much in this system for her. 'Penis envy' describes her resentment that her organ is not the main event. Although the sexual distinction is a social construction, it is consequent on the body, and in her eyes, it arises because of the body she has. Freudian theory describes her supposed chagrin at this 'narcissistic wound'. There are infinite hypothetical social orders which make some sense of the two human bodies and the two kinds of genitals, but Freud articulates the (common) sense that is made of them in a patriarchal one.[8]

Yet Freud must complain to Marie Bonaparte that 'the great question that has never been answered and which I have not been able to answer despite my thirty years of research into the feminine soul is "what does a woman want?"'. *I can't seem to satisfy her.* This is a *theoretical* problem; he can tell us quite strictly on his account what he wants and why – he wants the substitute he was promised for his first love-object, a reasonable facsimile of his mother (if the process has gone according to plan). But he cannot so firmly declare her desire.

He is naturally guilty of a certain amount of flirtation in the remark – perhaps the subject of woman cannot be canvassed without its becoming an erotic question. At the beginning of the lecture on 'Femininity';

'*To those of you who are women this will not apply, you are yourselves the problem*'! One can hear the jocularity as all in the audience titter – both sexes can take away a frisson.

The discussion of female sexuality becomes more vexed in later years. The problem passes to the next generation – Karen Horney, Melanie Klein, Helene Deutsch, Ernest Jones – but in terms of a theory which accounts for social roles as structures erected on an anatomical base, Freud's remains the more flexible even where his observations are apparently less 'friendly', as he puts it at the end of his lecture.

The outcome of Freud's sexual researches is that he is left unable to answer the question 'what does a woman want?', from within his theory. This is an interesting failure in a theory built on the hypothesised sexual wishes of female hysterics. Perhaps, in taking desire as the object of its investigation, the science of psychoanalysis guaranteed that its paradoxes would be fruitful. Feminine desire emerges as a symptom, not only on the theory, but *of the theory*; it remains a sticking point, repressed and unconscious – to put it in terms the theory itself proposes. In this, psychoanalysis demonstrates something, not only about desire, but exhibits something about theory.

Contesting psychoanalysis at this theoretical locus – the incoherence of its dealing with the literal 'woman' – has led feminism to a highly-coloured but oversimplified critique of Freud and his effects on the possible discourses of sexuality (and as we shall see, of Lacan). This is not to say that it is not appropriate to offer critique of modern therapeutic theory and practice. But the radical potential in Freudian theory, and thus its value for a politics of sexuality and gender, lies elsewhere, in its conception of the body as a place of historically-engendered pleasure and pain. That the process can fail is at least as important a feature of the theory as the account it gives of success. It gives us theoretical resources with which to reflect and anticipate differences.

5 Love

Tucked away among pieces of homely advice on the placing of the furniture and the fixing of the fee comes Freud's account of the transference – the 'Papers on technique'.[1] Transference is a concept that ostensibly relates to the practice of psychoanalysis, rather than the theory. But in fact, transference has a pivotal place in the theory, and cannot be contained to the area of practice. It is a relation with ontological as well as epistemological consequences.

In the glossary, *The Language of Psychoanalysis*, transference is defined as 'a process of actualisation of unconscious wishes' (Laplanche and Pontalis, 1973, 455). In the transference, 'infantile prototypes re-emerge and are experienced with a strong sensation of immediacy'. How and why is this a possibility? Precisely because *in transference we encounter experience*, i.e. how it comes about. 'The strong sensation of immediacy' is part of the shock of transference, and it is this aspect which has implications for what we call 'experience'. It is the unconscious in action.

Transference is 'an event whose strangeness Freud never tired of emphasising' – it has a relation to the uncanny, and to the compulsion to repeat. It seems uncanny because to see the terms of what one normally assumes to be given or natural – to watch it being fabricated and yet to experience its reality – is to have 'something come to light which should have remained hidden' (1919, 225). Experience is something we imagine happens to us, or that we encounter. Rarely do we have the privilege of experiencing the hand we have in it.

The concept of transference evolves from the pressure of the analytic situation itself. But of course in identifying it as a consequence of analysis, in these papers, Freud is forced to grant it is like real life, and it is a piece of real life. More specifically, it is a species of love, and can be explained therefore through the mechanism that explains love. 'The cure is effected by love', Freud tells us. That mechanism Freud outlines at the beginning of the 'Dynamics of transference':

> [e]ach individual, through the combined operation of his innate dis-
> position and the influences brought to bear on him during his early
> years, has acquired a specific method of his own in his conduct of his
> erotic life – that is, in the preconditions to falling in love which he lays
> down, in the instincts he satisfies and the aims he sets himself in the
> course of it. This produces what might be described as a stereotype
> plate (or several such), which is constantly repeated – constantly re-
> printed afresh – in the course of the person's life, so far as external
> circumstances and the nature of the love-objects accessible to him
> permit, and which is certainly not entirely insusceptible to change in
> the face of recent experiences.
>
> (1914, 99)

If we refer this to other parts of Freudian theory, to inquire where these
'stereotype plates' might come from, we realise that they belong to
certain ideas as they represent the instinctual, in the various phases of
sexual development; the idea of 'imagoes' belonging to the experiences
of infant love life. There are none stronger than the collection of images
that are introjected at the castration complex in the form of the super-
ego.

Freud goes on to point out that not all of these are conscious – there
are libidinal impulses that we know to be repressed, and whose pattern-
ing effect in experience is unknown to the individual, or unseen, even
though it forms a crucial part of the character of each action. These
erotic templates, particularly the unconscious ones, are seen operating
in the transference.

In virtue of their being repressed, such configurations have not had
the benefit of a modification by 'reality', says Freud, in the way that
other impressions from early experience have had, and so they persist in
our actions as impulses with infantile aims. Since they are repressed,
their original occurrences are not remembered but acted out in the
present; 'they persist as actualised impulses'. Behind transferential
action lies the conception of the instinct, its pressure, and its indirect
translation into conscious life.

> As long as the patient is in the treatment he cannot escape from this
> compulsion to repeat and in the end we understand that this is his
> way of remembering.
>
> (1914, 150)

In the transference, the patient, according to Freud's account, intro-
duces the doctor into one of the psychical series which he has already

formed (for example, into the father-imago or mother-imago). For this to happen, it can be inferred that we experience present love in relation to the original experiences of love, and that they provide a blueprint for later impulses in relation to object-choice and aim. It is not a description confined to the neurotic/therapeutic; since all love has its genesis in the directing of libido, then transference is only a pathological phenomenon in as much as it is manufactured in the therapeutic sphere and under circumstances which are 'excessive' to it.

For example, it seems likely that if transference is operative in the workplace it is more often consummated and called an 'affair'; and if it is animated between the priest and the postulant it is called a 'sin'. So what is exhibited in the transference in analysis is merely a specialised kind of libidinal action which is found in human relations generally. Freud himself mentions specifically the relation of teacher to pupil, and of confessor to congregation. But every relation is to some extent libidinal, and it is the part which strikes one as compulsive or excessive which marks the unconscious component, rather than its presence in any particular environment. Freud gives this idea its widest operation when he talks about the possibility of a fate neurosis in 'Beyond the pleasure principle'; he talks there about the repetition of experience's amounting to the habit of a lifetime, in a woman who complains of having nursed three husbands on their deathbeds (1920, 22).

Transference is a special case of love:

> In the first place it is provoked by the analytic situation; secondly, it is greatly intensified by the resistance, which dominates the situation; and thirdly, it is lacking to a high degree in a regard for reality, is less sensible, less concerned about consequences and more blind in its valuation of the loved person than we are prepared to admit in the case of normal love. We should not forget, however, that these departures from the norm constitute precisely what is essential about being in love.
>
> (1914, 168)

The tables are turned, and being in love itself is revealed as a kind of pathology, in as much as it is regarded as an elemental phenomenon which interrupts. 'People write their ideas of love on a separate page', as Freud expresses it. It is the departure from the rational law that is precisely what is valued about being in love, as Freud has seen. So he inverts the question about what is pathological in transference-love by arguing that being in love in ordinary life resembles abnormal mental phenomena.

The 'imagos' by which the individual repeats the series of feelings and actions in relation to another in the present, on the basis of the past, are not confined to the explicitly erotic, and are not all unconscious. It is through the sublimation of those structures, in a process analogous to metaphorical identification, that are discovered instinctual impulses acting in normal and necessary relations to the world. They have a common root:

> sympathy, friendship, trust, and the like, which can be turned to good account in our lives, are genetically linked with sexuality and have developed from purely sexual desires through a softening of their sexual aim.

(1914, 105)

Here emerges the Freudian thesis, that libidinal energy is modified in the service of culture. The production of cultural artefacts is an indirect expression of sexual desires; that modification, as sublimation to social ends, includes the production of knowledge, both in the accruing of personal understanding and experience, and the epistemophilia of the intellectual. In effect, each engagement in life contains libidinal material; and indeed if passionately pursued, this may be the very aspect which brings success – Freud notes that where the unconscious aim can be joined with conscious intent, the result can be extraordinary achievement. The metaphorical ambience of love takes us from libido to sociality and thence to 'life', to the instincts which oblige us to reach out to others for increase.

What is the difference between transference and love? Superficially it is 'anything which is excessive' – it is that part of any relation where libido protrudes. The process can be recognised as anything 'which exceeds in amount or nature anything which can be justified on sensible or rational grounds' (1914, 100). It is measured by excess, reaction to more than the present circumstances. But this is itself artificial; transference emerges in the confinement of two libidinal subjects to the roles of doctor, patient, teacher, pupil, since those roles are not complete expressions of the psychical possibilities of the individuals involved.

On another level, nothing seems more natural than to fall in love with the analyst, who is listening and attending in a careful way. The difference between transference and love is the difference between analysis and life. But the analysis, as an experience and as an institution, owes its paradoxical success to this artificial intimacy; to the creation under experimental conditions of a rapport normally experienced between people in natural love relations. And the result of this experiment is to lay bare the structure of character. It does so because the analyst, unlike lover or kin, does not engage with the behaviour as literal present, but instead *interprets* it as an exhibition of the past. And in engaging with the patient's actions (including declarations), the analyst does not participate in their enactment as he or she would in 'real world' relations (to do so would set up the interference of 'counter-transference').

The analyst interprets the action so that the patient can see the unconscious 'imago' behind it, and can come to recognise the pattern which has been set up. Interpreting the transference, like interpreting the dream, means understanding the 'primary process' thinking characteristic of the unconscious. In particular, the 'timeless' quality of the unconscious is exhibited in transference in the disregard of the distinction between past and present, between the original experience and the present opportunity. The unconscious knows love as a certain configuration, and enacts that configuration with each subsequent love-object. For the neurotic, since there is ambivalence in the way in which love is enacted, the analysis hypothesises that the experience underlying his or her erotic education was disturbing and painful.

Freud argues that it would be disingenuous for psychoanalysis to deny that the patient's love for her doctor is genuine (1914, 168). *She is in love; it is not fraudulent, it is artificial.* The consequences of that distinction are important for the analyst's response in the treatment. Because of the circumstances of the analysis, transference-love is arguably a more perfect expression of love in its essence than we meet with in ordinary life. It is allowed its pathological aspect. It is the very artificiality of the analytic situation which, like the hothouse, produces the most perfect blooms. What is transference if it can synthesise passions more excellent than those occurring naturally? The structure of analysis is peculiarly engaged with the unconscious 'imagos', and deliberately facilitates their action, the better to reconfigure them. The production of the transference-neurosis is essential to effecting the cure, Freud notes, and eventually all comes to be played out in the transference relation. It gives the neurosis its present and living example, it makes its 'case-study'; 'when all is said and done, it is impossible to destroy someone *in absentia* or *in effigie*' (1914, 108).

Transference then is more than a by-product of analysis; it becomes the vehicle of the treatment. It intrudes as a form of resistance, but as an essential one.[2] As a symptom, it implies 'conjuring up a piece of real life'. It is a piece of real experience, but one that has been made possible by 'especially favourable conditions' and it is of 'a provisional nature'. It may invoke behaviour which is 'inappropriate' and yet it may necessarily do so, in order for the analyst to use the excessive character for interpretation. It is provisional because the analyst is not entering into the transference at the level of its literal demand, which makes it a thoroughly 'one-sided' relation.

If this frustrates the patient's expectation, then in so doing *it questions the 'ontology' implied*. As such, Freud describes the transference as creating 'an intermediate region between illness and real life through which the transition from one to the other is made' (1914, 154). Analysis is characterised as a kind of twilight zone, in which standing orders are suspended and modification of the ground rules is accomplished; the re-working of the imagos is effected. But what does this synthetic experience of the analysis imply about real life? Simply, that experience is a synthetic matter; that there is manufacture. This puts paid to the idea of the elemental character of love. It can be modified and adapted, it can be experienced otherwise – the point of analysis is to bring about nothing less. Transference exhibits the path, or the process, by which experience is manufactured, by showing how a piece of the past is repeated in the present as experience, as a form of the past. We employ this kind of past memory, in order to produce the present.

Now psychical experience can be seen as a flow of libido following the specific forms it has been fashioned in, following its previous course. It can be seen how it can be forced to flow differently, in new terrain. So theoretically, *the past conditions the present* in this manufacture of experience. Analysis, by refusing the naturalism of that experience, also demonstrates how, out of a process of frustration, experience is modified by experience. Thus, analysis allows us to see, also, how *the present can condition the past*. This is the therapeutic aim.

What looks like technique or practice is profoundly connected to theory and indeed, without the concept of transference, psychoanalytic theory cannot be fully understood. Transference is possible because instinctual energy is a fluid affair. The vicissitudes of the instinct are recorded in the various moments of a sexual history: Freud visualises the result on a metaphor of stereotype plates, but also infers the possibility of tableaux of complementary roles, and also of their staging, which implies their repetition.[3]

Freud makes two assumptions about the nature of this libidinal action. In the first place, that the course of satisfaction is fixed, to a great extent, by the epochal formations of infancy, so that like a watercourse, energy continues to flow in those channels. To change the course calls for structural modifications and engineering. Nevertheless, the encounter of that landscape with the ever-changing agents of circumstance produces effects akin to weathering; there are natural forces which over time affect the shapes of those channels, and not all of these environmental influences need be as subtle as wind or waves. There is the psychical equivalent of earthquake and flood, as the war neuroses attest.[4]

Importantly, transference enters at the point at which the theory of psychical structure is put into the context of human life and lived experience. The apparatus of the topographical model, the turbine of the dynamic-economic, is now a veritable vehicle with its own living motion. While transference appears to go on in a local corner of Freud's writing, in fact it is a key to the theory and a demonstration of it. If the analyst actually can prompt the subject to reform the terms of his or her engagement – if, that is, someone can be led back to the past and led through it again to a different conclusion – and if one could re-make one's expectations of pleasure and re-order one's desires of others, then not only would one be able to 'change one's life', but the theory of how one came by those desires in the first place would be vindicated.

Desire is modified by contact with the external circumstance, like ionising metals exposed to the air. This is what Freud means by the 'reality principle'. How can this be? It is because this has always been the function of the mind, of consciousness, to bring desire into reality by making an experience of it. The whole apparatus, its layers and relations, are aimed at performing this manufacture, producing instinctual needs in a form capable of satisfaction. In virtue of this, Freud's theory does not present external circumstance as having a lien on reality. 'Reality' is the function of the ego, and is strictly a principle, not a fact – just as 'pleasure' is the principle for the id. *Reality is an experience* – this is the empiricist consequence. Reality means psychical reality (however 'unrealistic' it appears to other minds). This is how the terms of empiricism, ironically, have Freud trapped in the subjective. The reality is always limited to, as it is expressed by, its terms of representation.

And yet Freud is reaching for something more, here, for an intuition of the effect of something from outside, something of the external world intruding and compelling. When he considers this problem in other language, he can talk quite simply of people who have been *disappointed* by life, whose *expectations* of themselves and others made it unlikely they should ever be happy, and even perhaps of some who show fortitude in being able to bear the frustration of their desire by life, who can be *reconciled* to that. If we receive tutelage in desire from circumstance in the first place, then we must go on learning – this is Freud's everyday wisdom, that the human being needs to love and work.[5]

Knowledge is conceived of as the product of the interaction between the desires we have and the circumstances in which they seek satisfaction. Transference leads to an epistemological assertion that the acting-out of the representations of the past means that what is known produces new knowledge; for example, the hostile father-imago produces the conviction that 'the doctor hates me'. In that it is this very interaction which makes up experience – and if being is nothing other than experience – then in terms of the ontological, what transference brings about is precisely the *present*, circumstances of whose character it is accurate to report: 'I am in love with the doctor'.

The consequences of that include conceding the importance for epistemology and ontology of the *interaction* of psyches in the manner of transference – but this will become clearer in reading Lacan. But we can see from the plasticity of the notions of past and present, how 'rereading' experience becomes possible, and how experience itself may be changed.

6 Language

To demonstrate the affinities between psychoanalysis and their own concerns, many contemporary writers refer to certain totemic moments in the theory, such as the essay on the uncanny or the death drive, or point to fetish objects like the dream or the mystic writing pad. But it is also possible to explore conceptual schemes in Freudian theory that foreshadow contemporary philosophies; to ask, *is there a psychoanalysis of theory?*[1]

Freud's popularism may have served his own purposes in advancing the fame of psychoanalysis, but it does not always serve him theoretically. The positivism of later writing, in the 'New introductory lectures', for example, is at odds with the adventurous tenor of the 'metapsychological' papers written between 1915 and 1923, in which the theory of psychoanalysis is worked out.[2] There is an evolution, or perhaps an involution, from the young man who reports wanting 'only philosophical knowledge', to the (self)contempt of 'An autobiographical study' which desires to keep only an 'unembarrassed' mind.[3]

In 'Beyond the pleasure principle', Freud talks of science as a figurative language. Having carved up the psychical territory in that paper, between the life and death instincts, and having told a long story about the vicissitudes of these instincts, he finds certain inelegancies in the account. He comments:

> We need not feel greatly disturbed in judging our speculation upon the life and death instincts by the fact that so many bewildering and obscure processes occur in it – such as one instinct being driven out by another or an instinct turning from the ego to an object, and so on. This is merely due to our being obliged to operate with the scientific terms, that is to say with the figurative language, peculiar to psychology ... We could not otherwise describe the processes in

question at all, and indeed we could not have become aware of them.

(1920, 60)

He presents the problem as one in which the particular figures do not offer the desirable consistency. But an imperfect tool is better than none – Freud claims to have adopted hypotheses as required in order to advance the understanding of what is happening before his eyes. Since it has had to be deduced by a process of indirect hypothesis, it may well be imperfect; nevertheless, without adopting these models which project the theory forward he could not have brought certain occurrences to scientific observation at all. The theoretical task then includes the synthesis of apparently incommensurate observations through a process of metaphorisation.

> The deficiencies in our description would probably vanish if we were already in a position to replace the psychological terms by physiological or chemical ones. It is true that they too are only part of a figurative language; but it is one with which we have long been familiar and which is perhaps a simpler one as well.
>
> (*ibid.*)

There is nothing privileged in their access to reality; the claim of the figurative discourse of chemistry or physics is on the basis of its being *better known*, and of readers having a greater facility with its narratives and metaphors. Freud here depicts the theoretical discourse in functional terms: which of the tropes will better shape the subject under discussion.[4]

In 'Instincts and their vicissitudes', he describes a somewhat similar process in terms of what postulations are required in order to pursue the formulations of a science. The notion of the instinct, for example, is allegorical for psychology, since the source of the instinct is not directly observed in psychical life. It is in the very nature of the instinct to have this grounding in the somatic, i.e. non-psychological. Psychology is from the beginning figurative, in relation to the instinct. And yet the instinct has its representatives, i.e. its representations, in psychology through which it becomes known. The fact that those representations are themselves often unconscious only doubles the difficulty of observation and increases the indirectness of our relation to them.

In order, therefore, to defend as knowledge what he is producing, Freud is obliged to be more flexible about what can be said about what can be seen.

> We have often heard it maintained that sciences should be built up on clear and sharply defined basic concepts. In actual fact no science,

not even the most exact, begins with such definitions. The true beginning of scientific activity consists rather in describing phenomena and then in proceeding to group, classify and correlate them. Even at the stage of description it is not possible to avoid applying certain abstract ideas to the material in hand, ideas derived from somewhere or other but certainly not from the new observations alone.

(1915, 117)

The level of scientific description is not protected by any empirical transparence; it can allow for other kinds of description to run alongside. This allows a legitimate scientific description, in neurophysiological terms say, without invalidating a description offered in the language of psychology. It will not rule out more mystical or artistic explorations of the subject (which indeed Freud often draws on).

Such ideas – which will later become the basic concepts of the science – are still more indispensable as the material is further worked over ... They must at first necessarily possess some degree of indefiniteness; there can be no question of any clear delimitation of their content. So long as they remain in this condition, we come to an understanding about their meaning by making repeated references to the material of observation from which they appear to have been derived, but upon which, in fact, they have been imposed.

(*ibid.*)

These ideas have come from 'somewhere or other', but not from the 'observations alone'. *From where do these ideas, which are to become its basic concepts, come?* Freud describes: 'Thus, strictly speaking, they are in the nature of conventions'. At the kernel of the theory, convention interacts with observation. Strictly, it becomes a circular process; at a certain point, the observed material refines the concept that made the observation possible. Any discourse, even the most literally factual, has made that circular movement, by finding its premises in its conclusion, according to this view. The only error would be the naivety which imagines that, as a result of this, it is a 'discovery'.

The advance of knowledge does not tolerate rigidity even in definitions, and Freud cites physics as 'an excellent illustration' – an appeal to the discursive operation of a hard science, as a defence of the way his own science is proceeding.[5] In itself, this is not a disinterested process; theoretical discourse is an interaction between the needs of articulation and the dictates of the observed.

The instinct, Freud concludes, is 'a conventional basic concept of this kind'. If scientific concepts are in the nature of conventions, then the idea of an instinct becomes so *par excellence*, for it remains an effect-ively contentless node around which a whole account is assembled, describing forces in a dynamic system in psychical terms. The instinct begins as a shadow; what we know of it is always indirect and a result of what we need to know about it in order to account for psychical manifestations.

When Freud speaks, in 'Beyond the pleasure principle', of sciences as being expressed as figurative languages, he is not suggesting that what is thus being described is a mere fiction. But these conventions bring with them figurative expectations, and it is Freud's complaint that narratives that are inappropriate or implausible are having to be improvised (for example, in 'one instinct turning around onto itself' and so on) precisely because the genre lacks the 'means of representation'. This was the third principle of dream interpretation proposed in ch. 6 of 'The inter-pretation of dreams', and a necessary consideration in reading the un-conscious in general. Perhaps Freud would prefer to tell the story as a physiological one, or as a chemical one, and yet, the justification of the psychological figures lies in the comment that, without them, certain theoretical possibilities would remain obscured ('we could not have become aware of them at all'). This gives a formative place to the figures of psychoanalysis as a particular kind of theoretical 'sight'.

The intriguing consequence of this 'aesthetic' of scientific theory is that were one to render the instinct, for example, in physiological or chemical terms, it would not thereby tell the 'real' story of which psy-choanalysis were an allegory. At best, it would offer the familiarity and simplicity of its own figures. The reader, educated in the ways of the scientific genres, would see the virtue of it in terms much like the advan-tage gained from using symbolic notation over natural grammar – it brings conceptual clarity, but is not thereby 'truer' of the relation it illustrates.

Freud presents this view of scientific theory in defence specifically of the psychoanalytic narrative of the instinct. But it can be extended to better comprehend the nature of his 'metapsychology' itself. Freud proposes the term for an account that 'leads behind consciousness':[6] a psychology that comprehends the unconscious nature of the mental, and indeed the structures in the mind which account for its psychology. Strictly, it will be a hypothesis of what must lie behind the observed psychology.

He defines it further in the paper on 'The unconscious'. At a certain point in the essay, in commenting on the structure of the psyche in terms of three possible aspects – the 'topographical', the 'dynamic' and the 'economic' – Freud claims that to account for observed phenomena under the three regimes is what it would be to do metapsychology.[7] In effect, the metapsychology is to be governed by these three figures.

The 'Papers on metapsychology' are made more intriguing by the postulation of the loss (perhaps the destruction) of several of them (1915, 105). Freud often expresses an ambivalence about philosophy, and at times the distaste extends to the task of his metapsychology. In answer to Lou Andreas-Salomé's query 'where is your meta-psychology?', Freud writes: '[i]n the first place it remains unwritten. Working over material systematically is not possible for me. The fragmentary nature of my observations and the sporadic character of my ideas will not permit it' (Pfeiffer, 1972, 95). The comments suggest that he does not consider it his obligation to be systematic; he defends himself from the claims of theory with the empirical duty that comes from observation and from practice. He does not confess to this fragmentary nature as though it were a disability, but more as the virtue of being first and foremost an observer.

The limiting factor – or perhaps the creative edge – of psychoanalysis has been that the unconscious is an object that can be observed only indirectly, in failed repressions, in what escaped and has become conscious. To read the activities of this other psychical space, which becomes the foundational space, has always been an operation of induction. Freud likens it in another lecture to the postulation of the core of the earth; he specifically aligns his study with sciences that have the same problem, geology and astronomy, the observations of their object taking place through a medium.[8] But, as Freud there descibes it, not all indirect evidence is superstition. No one doubts the reality described by the geologist or the astronomer, even when they refer to the impenetrable event, the distant past, of which we could never have 'direct' knowledge.

If metapsychology aims at an explanation of the structure of the psyche, and an account into which observations can be fitted, naturally this raises immediately the problem of observation. In describing his metapsychology through the figures of the topographical, dynamic and economic – which relate to polarities that govern instinctual vicissitude – Freud does not attempt to resolve their different perspectives, but rather appeals to their very fragmentation as evidence of probity. This, too, was a guide to interpretation of the dream: suspecting its own explanations, to have confidence in the moment that seemed most obscure.

The 'topographical' depicts the parts of the mind as related in a metaphorical 'space'. The 'first' topography, from 'The interpretation of dreams', showed consciousness, the preconscious and the unconscious represented as an apparatus. The 'second' topography, offered in 'The ego and the id', relates three different terms – id, ego and super-ego – in a different configuration (1923, 24). In the topographical figure – perhaps the most naive way of conceiving of the structure if the mind – an attempt is made to locate materially the theoretical representations in relation to each other – although not to solve the question of where they lie literally in the mind/body, since the attempt to understand the mind as a physical entity is a question of anatomy.

The economic model depicts the psychical as a system driven by instinctual energy – the distribution of energy in the system defines differences between conscious and unconscious as differences in energy. In 'The unconscious', the conflict between these figures gives rise to the question, is the difference between conscious and unconscious a difference in psychic locality? or is it a change in psychical character or quality, as a result of quantities of energy moving through the system? (1915, 175–6).

This provokes a third figure, that of the dynamic, which accounts for the psychical phenomena in terms of an exchange of values and forces. The dynamic view depicts the psychical as animated by the contest of heterodox forces which resolve, vector-like, in the direction of compromise. The dynamic view also lends itself to mythologies, the psychical agencies frequently personified, or lent a political or social nuance as readily as a mechanical one. For example, in the analogy Freud evokes of marriage between ego and id, social relations are projected onto psychical operations in the portrait given of the ego's 'dependent relations'.[9]

All three figures assume the postulation of an original state of tension in the human psyche, which is elaborated according to a still more striking figure in 'Beyond the pleasure principle', as the striving of the life and death instincts against each other. Behind this stands a dialectic metaphor, of thesis and antithesis which continually resolve in a further state of affairs. If there is a possibility of theoretical commitment to dialectical thought in psychoanalysis, it lies here. *The resolution of tension is proposed as the very function of the mind*; in 'Instincts and their vicissitudes', Freud postulates 'the nervous system is an apparatus which has the function of getting rid of the stimuli that reach it, or of reducing them to the lowest possible level' (1915, 120).

What, then, is metapsychology? As Laplanche and Pontalis describe it, 'Metapsychology constructs an ensemble of conceptual models which are more or less far-removed from empirical reality' (Laplanche and Pontalis, 1973, 249). They dwell on the reference in this neologism to 'metaphysics', which they note is not a simple parallel. In many places, and explicitly in discussions of the dreamwork of 'secondary revision', metapsychology proposes itself as the *antidote* of metaphysics:

> [I]n a significant passage, he defines metapsychology as a scientific endeavour to redress the constructions of 'metaphysics'. He sees these – like superstitious beliefs or certain paranoiac delusions – as projecting what in reality are the properties of the unconscious on to forces in the outside world.
>
> (*ibid.*)[10]

But if we take this back to the accusation against metaphysics, that it projects psychical structures onto a supernatural reality, can we nevertheless sufficiently differentiate the scientific process from this? We can ask whether we have a case of introjection, where structures from an external world are taken into a conception of the mental? In as much as it is the imposition of conventions on perceptions of the real, it does not seem different in kind perhaps from the projection there denigrated: in both cases, an interpreting of signs through *a priori* conceptions.

Metapsychology, then, reverses the action of metaphysics. In discussing secondary revision, in 'The interpretation of dreams', Freud notes that it is provided with much of its apparent coherence from readymade structures in psychical life: phantasies, of which the 'day dream' is the classic case. The secondary revision often borrows these essentially wishful narrative structures for its dreamwork. A parallel can be made with the 'conventions borrowed from one knows not where'. Such a perspective makes of metaphysics a tendentious, even a wishful, activity. Indeed, writes Freud:

> The thing that distinguishes and at the same time reveals this part of the dream-work is its *purpose*. This function behaves in the manner which the poet [Heine] maliciously ascribes to philosophers: it fills up the gaps in the dream-structure with shreds and patches.
>
> (1900, 490)

The secondary revision (as deputy of rationality and conscious life) desires to comprehend. But if this is the problem with metaphysics, how can metapsychology avoid being hoist with its own petard, in projecting onto the supposed observations of mental phenomena the prefabricated schemas of the unconscious, which is to say, its desires?

Looking back to the description of scientific formulation offered in 'Instincts and their vicissitudes', where hypotheses coming from 'one knows not where' are imposed on the observation, and which serve as 'conventions' for conceptualising at all; such prefabricated positions seem reminiscent of the readymade phantasies described as a feature of the secondary revision, and do at least potentially amount to narratives. Is theory necessarily secondary revision? Can one do otherwise in theory than desire coherence? It is not that scientific postulates and religious convictions are the same thing for Freud; it is that on Freud's own description of the operations they share a common root, that which also was revealed at work in dreams: the fashioning of experience through desire.

Science is for Freud, one suspects, an advance on metaphysics, an intellectual development. As infantile sexuality is to mature sexuality, so superstition and religion ('occultism') is to science and reason: vestigially present but definitively transformed. (This is echoed in 'Civilization and its discontents' when he suggests that sexuality itself is a psychic function in a process of involution in the human species (1930, 105).) The role of metaphysics and philosophy in this is more ambiguous. But it seems that Freud must approach the view, however unfriendly to his own theoretical efforts, that all theory is governed by these interior narratives.

In itself, metapsychology is no antidote to metaphysics, since it proposes the old saw of empiricism, projecting structures from the external world onto the observations of the psyche. But perhaps it is not as metapsychology that psychoanalysis can antidote the projections of a metaphysics. Perhaps it is only as an interpretative procedure, as a method of reading, that psychoanalysis shows the unconscious at work in any conscious projection (even in its own).

If Freud presents the case for the figurative character of scientific representations, he also provides a halting argument from which one might develop a corollary: the material character of all our representations. Remarks in the metapsychological papers lead directly to Lacan's preoccupation with 'the signifier', and provide a good place from which to proceed toward these foreign formulations of Freud.

There is in Freud the suggestion that *there is something in the act of representation itself which is consciousness*. This argument proposes that language links theory to consciousness, by something more than *analogy*. Freud tells us the difference between conscious and unconscious thought depends on the relation between word and thing. In the paper on 'The unconscious', in interpreting the actions of a patient in a case of schizophrenia, Freud describes the obsessive squeezing of blocked pores of the skin as having a meaning for the patient associated with the castration complex: the expelling of material representing the idea of ejaculation, and the resulting hole suggesting the vagina (1915,

196–204). This case is uncharacteristic of hysteria, Freud notes, since the pores on the face are not sufficiently isomorphic with the vagina; the hysteric might be expected to relate the unconscious ideas to a part of the body more like the vagina in reality (a 'hole', for example, like the mouth).

But there is a level at which the pores of the skin can be likened to the vagina – at the level of the linguistic, where 'a hole is a hole'. *The association happens at the level of words, not things.* One of the characteristics for the schizophrenic, then, is the taking of the word for a thing, and making use of the word in its aspect as an object in reality.

In another case, a woman, who can give an account of what her language means and is therefore not hysteric for her meaning is not repressed, complains that her eyes are twisted, because her lover is an 'eye-twister', which is to say, untrustworthy; the association she proposes is once again verbal and not physical. Similarly, in two cases Freud notes of a psychical disturbance which is represented by the pulling on and off of stockings; the obsessional neurotic pulls the stocking off and on as a compulsive mime of masturbation, and an undoing or denial of it, but a schizophrenic becomes anxious because he must pull apart the *stitches* in order to perform the task, opening holes in the fabric. Freud notes the difference in their relations to the hole and its associations. While for the neurotic the action of inserting the foot in the sock is a relation between the dreaded action and the everyday, for the psychotic it is not the whole sock which represents literally a 'hole', but its tiny components, the stitches, which are related 'metaphorically'.

On the assumption that psychoses and neuroses manifest unconscious disturbances, Freud infers from this that what is collapsed in psychosis is that part of mental functioning that distinguishes the word-presentation from the thing-presentation, the symbol from the perception. Whereas in neurosis, the repressed idea is a thing-presentation from which the word-presentation, the ability to 'think' it, has been withdrawn.

We now seem to know all at once what the difference is between a conscious and an unconscious presentation. The two are not, as we supposed, different registrations of the same content in different psychical localities, nor yet different functional states of cathexis in the same locality; but the conscious presentation comprises the presentation of the thing plus the presentation of the word belonging to it, while the unconscious is the presentation of the thing alone.

(1915, 201)

Using the word as a representative of the thing, and to stand for (or even, perhaps, to 'name') the image, becomes what it means to make something conscious. In the unconscious, images are primarily events; in their hallucinatory character, they offer themselves as candidates for experience. Thus, they are credited primordially as 'things', and it is only the operation of the preconscious which shows them to be symbolic.[11] On the Freudian account, the unconscious is proposed as taking into itself images of its objects, and treating those images as any other sensory experience, as if they were 'real'. Under the influence of the preconscious, they can be presented in the mind as representative, and thus enter into the discriminating style of thought which is consciousness. In 'The ego and the id' Freud makes the hypothesis clearer:

> The part played by word presentations now becomes perfectly clear. By their interposition internal thought processes are made into perceptions. It is like a demonstration of the theorem that all knowledge has its origin in external perception. When a hypercathexis of the process of thinking takes place, thoughts are *actually* perceived – as if they came from without – and are consequently held to be true.
>
> (1923, 23)

By this route are *representations made real*, presented as things in themselves, or rather, in their thingly aspect, through the link between somatic and psychical which is the sensory event.

In theoretical terms, psychosis can now be structurally related to the loss of 'reality function'; what has been lost is the ability to appreciate the difference between the word and the thing, and to use them *in simultaneous senses*. The loss of the distinction between conscious and unconscious thought implies a loss of distinction among mental events, all of which are sensory events, those which arise from internal images and those from external. The result is a disturbance in the distinction between illusion and reality. The property of the preconscious has been to unite the notion of the word as a thing with the word as a symbol. For the schizophrenic, paradoxically, everything must appear in its aspect as thing – and thus, he has no defence against 'reality'; everything is alive. The woman, while sitting in church, 'has to wriggle', she reports, because she has to 'change her position' – she must find one less awkward since her lover has placed her in a compromising position.

The hysteric, in a similar position, cannot express the thought as an idea at all – in consequence, her thoughts have become real in that they have become a somatic experience.

The remarks on theory and the remarks in the theory about the status of the word-presentation lead us to imagine that there is something in the act of representation itself which is consciousness. It is that which manages to define reality and 'hold it still' for the purposes of perception, to make perception of it. The process that has been described for theory – in finding a concept one knows not where and in refining it – is the same kind of process as is being described here, presenting the word as an actual perception in order for the unconscious to express itself. This makes the line 'we could not have perceived these things without it' a switch point in Freud's conception, the line that links his understanding of what is happening in representation in general with that of theoretical representation.

The making-real of the presentation in the mind is the same idea as the making-real of the theoretical presentation on the observed material. Experience, 'literally', is a function of mental representation, whatever else it is. Experience is first and foremost, a sensoral event, a material event, in the body. If ideas are events before they are anything else, then 'reality' is a product of the body before anything else – the external world, ironically, is not even ontologically prior to our perceiving it, although it forms part of the transaction of that ontology and that perception.

In consequence, the whole project of empirical science belongs to the body, its mental agent and the advent of its experience. This is far from a facile faith in a common world, and it is also not one which makes an idealism of reality (or worse, an ideology of it). Since Freud conceives of experience as based on hallucination, then it is genuinely representation that consciousness endows. The disturbance of this process, 'the reality function', produces for the schizophrenic the internal as perception; for the hysteric the opposite, a barrier to internal perception.[12]

This arises conceptually from the commitment with which Freud began: that the mental is in the first place an event. The word, the wish, the truth and the lie are all at some level of the same order – they are mental images and this is how we experience them. Consciousness is conceived on the model of sense-perception – indeed explicitly so, by 'The ego and the id', which philosophically produces an 'atomism'.

It is this facility which is manifest in the transference, and in its widest generality is that which produces for psychoanalysis the past, the present and the future – the continuity of identity for a psychical series which is no more than a myriad of moments. Thus, we also see why time is a product of consciousness, and why, in the unconscious, things are timeless.

As empirical, representation becomes central to psychology because it allows for the revivifying of the image in actual experience. But representation is also the conjunction by which Freud's theory has lent itself to philosophies which seem far removed from Hume.

7   Knowledge

At the beginning of the seminar of 1964, published as *The Four Fundamental Concepts of Psychoanalysis*, Lacan asks of psychoanalysis whether it can be called a science – or better, whether it can be called a religion, given that he has been 'ex-communicated' by the International Association and barred from training analysts.

But his way of putting the question raises the prior problem of distinguishing science from religion, a difficulty he does not extricate psychoanalysis from. As definitions of science, he proposes two possibilities: that a science has an object; or at least that a science has a field. He argues the first, however, cannot be sustained since the objects of sciences change (witness the difference between modern physics and its precursors). But the second – knowing that praxis delimits a field, to ask whether it is at the level of the field that the modern scientist, 'who is not a man who knows a lot about everything, is to be specified' – is not enough to define science, since 'this definition might be applied very well, for example, to the mystical experience' (Lacan, 1977b, 7–9).

Psychoanalysis, at any rate, is the vexed case of a science because in it there is properly no way of avoiding the question, 'what is the analyst's desire?' – like alchemy, which required 'the purity of the soul of the operator' in the operation. Lacan notes that this question is left outside the limits of the field in modern sciences: the *subject* of science is avoided. The desire of the physicist – for example, of Oppenheimer – provokes a crisis when raised – and even then, this is considered a political and not a scientific crisis. But psychoanalysis cannot leave the analyst's desire outside the limits of its field; it is instantiated in the training analysis whose whole motive is to discover the (potential) *analyst's* desire. This must be done, in order to unmask the transferences that operate for the analyst.

However, one way in which psychoanalysis is science, for Lacan's polemic, is in its membership of a group of studies which are producing 'a revolution in knowledge': those structuralist studies which treat language as their object (1977, 149). Theory and praxis are linked in this. Knowledge is built out of the relation between the subject and its other, including its objects, and Lacan's conception of the mirror stage condenses the foregoing questions – of science, of religion and of structuralism – in the one scene: the subject seeing itself in the mirror.

The paper on the 'mirror stage' provides an abstract of Lacan's translation of psychoanalysis from a science of the mind to a philosophy of the subject. His engagement with philosophy and the philosophy of his milieu is on display in this paper – an interest registered from the first paragraph where he writes that the formation of the 'I' 'is an experience that leads us to oppose any philosophy directly issuing from the *cogito*'. It gives advance warning of an engagement with Descartes and the 'philosophical subject'.

The philosophical strength of the mirror stage is to open up the possibility of psychical reality as a 'virtual reality'; to put in play the metaphor of the virtual. An innovative elaboration of Freud – at the surface of the mind–body, the instinctual pressure creates a signifiying field, a space of signs. Its inaugural symbol is the *imago* of oneself, the mirror-image, and its narrative is the 'mirror stage'.

The function of the mirror stage is 'a particular case of the function of the *imago*, which is to establish a relation between the organism and its reality – or, as they say, between the *Innenwelt* and the *Umwelt*' (1977, 4). Proposing this as a virtual space, Lacan carries through Freud's intuition, the conception of the psychical as that place of negotiation or compromise between the libidinal energy of the instinct and its representation. He makes the case in the metaphor of the mirror.

> this conception originated in a feature of human behaviour illuminated by a fact of comparative psychology. The child, at an age when he is for a time, however short, outdone by the chimpanzee in instrumental intelligence, can nevertheless already recognise as such his own image in a mirror . . .
>
> This act, far from exhausting itself, as in the case of the monkey, once the image has been mastered and found empty, immediately rebounds in the case of the child in a series of gestures in which he experiences in play the relation between the movements assumed in the image and the reflected environment, and between this virtual complex and the reality it reduplicates – the child's own body, and the persons and things, around him.
>
> (1977, 1)

'In a flutter of jubilant activity', Lacan writes, describing the relation of the infant to this moment. It evokes the experience of pleasure in the forming image of self; it is necessarily a libidinal movement. Lacan spells that out when he describes it as disclosing a 'libidinal dynamism'. But the notion of the virtual also captures the narcissism which preoccupies him, and an 'ontological structure of the human world' in which knowledge is paranoic. Knowledge is related strictly to the theoretical structure he gives to paranoia: i.e., for Lacan, knowledge goes through the question of the other, and desire disturbs it. Far from completing oneself as autonomous, knowledge extends the glamour of certainty in exactly those situations where one is lost in the other. What seems to have originated with the 'I' comes from the other – the prototypic example is the reflection which, while it is called the 'I', arose in the mirror and, more broadly, in the (virtual) world.

Knowledge is paranoia *par excellence* since it is the 'mistaken' belief in one's own projections as literal objects outside the self, whereas they are in effect products of the relation of the inside to the outside. Its implication is more ambivalent, still – the *méconnaissance* is not even that what appears to come from the 'I' comes from the other, it is that it comes as the *reflection of one in the other*, and thus, it comes from their connection, their relation. This is the root of the problem; self and other, while as terms can be distinguished as an oppositional pair and even described as a relation, are not strictly separable.

'But the important point is that this form situates the agency of the ego, before its social determination, in a fictional direction' (1977, 2). For Lacan at this moment a nature is instated; in the very possibility of the permanence that the *imago* offers in comparison to the sensate fluctuation of the experience of the body, an 'alienating destination is prefigured', to use his phrase. Something is made rigid, which keeps the subject from itself as much as represents the subject to itself. As a consequence, the 'discordance in one's reality is of significance for the formation of neuroses or psychoses, and for the success or failure of this synthesis of the "I"'.

The first person, the 'I', as a universal piece of grammar, stabilises as it synthesises the subject's identity. But whatever the success of that dialectical operation, the 'institutionalising of subjectivity',[1] and of the subject subjected to it, the result will be 'asymptotic'. The 'discordance with his own reality' is a condition of that ego-identity. Indeed, Lacan seems not to be as interested in the synthesis as cure as in the possibility of effecting a symbolic communication between inside and outside which will represent both. It will not necessarily be a universal nor objective effect, conforming to a normal social 'ego' – this is the basis of his angry disagreement with American psychotherapies.[2]

The infant's mirror-image 'is still pregnant with the correspondences that unite the I with the statue in which man projects himself', 'the pygmalion he attempts to make of himself', 'with the phantoms that dominate him'. Lacan lists some of these projections: in dreams, the fortress and the disintegration into a body in pieces; the 'fragilisation', the hysterical body and its 'imaginary anatomy'; the automaton 'in which, in an ambiguous relation, the world of his own making tends to find completion', the prosthetic of technology. Writes Lacan, *'the mirror image would seem to be the threshold of the visible world'*. Lacan sets up the psychical field as virtual, and 'human knowledge is determined in that "little reality"'.

Two other pictures are offered in Lacanian theory of the relation of the subject to the external world through its objects. The trajectory of the drive is sketched in Figure 2, the 'itinerary of the drive'. The circuit of the drive is imagined as coming out of its source in the body into the external world, so that the object **(a)** (that piece of the world which answers the subject's demand) is captured in the noose of the trajectory. But it also returns, and this is the aim of the drive; the circuit re-enters the body as pleasure, as satisfaction, which puts the goal not with the object but back with the source. Freud designates the instinct as a

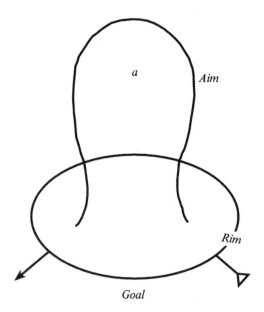

Figure 2 Lacan's 'itinerary of the drive'.
Source: Lacan, 1977b, 178.

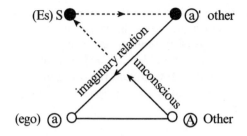

Figure 3 Lacan's *Schéma L.*
Source: Lacan, 1977, 193.

threshold concept; here, in order to become part of the circuit, the object becomes postulated as a representation or as a sign.

As in the mirror, this depicts a part of the world being returned narcissistically to the subject. When Lacan says 'all knowledge is paranoic', he is clearly suggesting that the influence of the other (**a**) is always indirect, and uncannily disturbed by the narcissism of the goal. The hermetic relation is clarified in another picture of the subject, given in the '*Schéma L*' (Figure 3). The relation between the ego and its objects is designated by the line between **a** and **a**' (l'autre), the other. The unconscious is the capitalised **A**, the Other; the speech or conscious discourse, which the subject knows as itself, is designated **S**. The quadrature, spread over four terms, thus shows the subject completing itself in the other. But not completely; one of the terms lies 'outside' the subject, as a representation. The **a**' is an image of the outside which is incorporated in the subject. The model suggests a dynamism, the ego constantly moving through the world, continually seeking confirmation of itself. It can be superimposed on the diagram of the itinerary of the drive, pushing the identifications out and back in pursuit of the goal, which is always a yield of pleasure. And both depictions can be translated into the mirror-metaphor. If the line between ego and other were to be tilted so as to reveal itself as a plane, then it could be seen to be the mirror; if it were to be a surface not an edge, it would be seen as a reflecting one.[4]

> The *mirror stage* is a drama whose internal thrust is precipitated from insufficiency to anticipation – and which manufactures for the subject ... the succession of phantasies that extends from a fragmented body-image to a form of its totality that I shall call orthopaedic ... Thus, to break out of the circle of the *Innenwelt* into the *Umwelt* generates the inexhaustible quadrature of the ego's verifications.
>
> (1977, 4)[5]

As in Freud, the metapsychology condensed in these images presupposes a continuity or history; in Lacan, from the fragmented body experience to the orthopaedic *imago* of the mirror, the kernel of the 'assumption of the armour of an alienating identity' which structures the subject's entire mental development. It is around the precipitate of this mirror-image that character is constructed, the ego formed in its layers of identifications with the other.

The mirror stage is not only the image of love for Lacan, but also that of knowledge. The first distinction is libidinal for Lacan, as for Freud; the creation of the self creates not only one's other – which is to say, one's lover – but is notably an *intellectual* operation.[6] The order of the imaginary is the field of the relations between the ego and its objects, not only love-objects but also conceptions. In knowledge no less than in love, it is identity that is negotiated – a risky business, the penalty of which is bodily disintegration.

The mirror stage 'turns the *I* into that apparatus for which every instinctual thrust constitutes a danger, even though it should correspond to a natural maturation' (1977, 5). With the establishment of the subject's structure, the movement between ego and objects is not merely a necessary but a dangerous one, threatening to collapse identity even while it is crucial to the constitution of it. This depicts the subject in an unhappy position.

Lacan considers the *fort-da* game, described by Freud in 'Beyond the pleasure principle'. In that game, the infant rehearses the loss and the finding again of a cotton reel tied to a piece of string. 'This reel is not the mother . . . it is a small part of the subject that detaches itself from him while still remaining his, still retained. This is the place to say, in imitation of Aristotle, that man thinks with his object' (1977b, 62). This illustrates brilliantly the conceptual link between love and knowledge; as it is only through the other that one becomes oneself, the other must become a signifier *of that*, and what the other signifies, then, is invariably a self-referential proposition.

The account of the *fort-da* game occurs in a discussion of death and repetition which links it to the predicament of self and other which the child is spelling out in the game. The mother's absence does not prompt the vigilance for her return so much as anxiety over her disappearance, a drama which Lacan sees as staged around the subject and not the object, the condition of subjectivity. 'For the game of the cotton-reel is the subject's answer to what the mother's absence has created on the frontier of his domain . . . namely a *ditch*, around which one can only play at jumping' (*ibid.*).

Repetition is the string, representing the obligation to go through the object to gain satisfaction, and to continue to do so. Lacan envisages this as a bond and even as a shackle, but his depiction of that original pain in store for the subject in relation to its object is dictated by the postulation of an already-desiring subject – one who desires autonomy from the object. This desire is a profound commitment of the Lacanian view, diagnosed as the specifically masculine desire in the conception of the phallus.

The relation between the ego and its objects is truly ambivalent; in Lacan, the notion of the death drive is recast schematically into a view of narcissism as generating both love and aggression, and the possibility of violence.[7] The alarming scenario reveals the common root of love and knowledge, and refers to the circumstances of psychosis. For, as Laplanche and Pontalis define it,

> Fundamentally, psychoanalysis sees the common denominator of the psychoses as lying in a primary disturbance of the libidinal relation to reality; the majority of manifest symptoms, and particularly delusional construction, are accordingly treated as secondary attempts to restore the link with objects.
>
> (Laplanche and Pontalis, 1973, 370)

Thus, if knowledge is paranoid, it must be that the knowing subject is already in the position of the psychotic, the 'libidinal relation to reality' disturbed by the very nature of things. This is the predicament contemplated in the mirror – it poses the irreducible problem of *the experience of the outside for the inside*. Knowledge encounters this as a definitional condition. Lacan is aware of this epistemological predicament, when he writes:

> I do not accept Duhem's demand that every science should refer to a unitary, or world, system – a reference that is always in fact more or less idealist, since it is a reference to the need of identification. I would even go so far as to say that we can dispense with the implicit transcendent element in the position of the positivist, which always refers to some ultimate unity of all the fields.
>
> (1977b, 8)[8]

If knowledge and delusion flow from a common libidinal spring, what can distinguish them? Lacan's rhetoric is not designed to do so; on the contrary, his whole metaphorics aims at intensifying their paradoxical similarity. It cannot be possible to make such a distinction through an appeal to the 'outside', since this will always have been routed through the 'inside' in advance. The distinction is insoluble to the extent that the *imago* in the mirror is always both self and other.

The subject emerges from its surroundings, like the figure from the ground. It takes a mirror to offer a reflection – but it must have something to reflect. The mirror is a tantalising metaphor for the process – it entrenches the fictional, the optical illusion and the confidence trick as ontological figures. But perhaps it cannot give Lacan the model he is seeking, for the circulation of the inside through the outside. The mirror begins not as a signifying reality in its own right but as dependent on that which it reflects, and of which it makes up an unseen part. As a metaphor, the mirror emphasises the anxiety about the truth or falsity of ideas, and shows the ego's conviction of knowledge in pure inversion, as a radical doubt and mistrust.

This produces an unseen difficulty for Lacan when he comes to use the notion of the virtual in a subjective scene. While the mirror is no original, the mind is active in its own interpretations, bringing them to pass. The figure makes it paradoxically hard to value the diversity the theory allows, since there is a 'true' and a 'real' shadowing the scene, albeit negatively. In effect, the mirror is judgemental, as is the rhetoric of the fictional, the imaginary, *méconnaissance* and *trompe l'oeil*, competing with a view of the subject which promotes the idiosyncratic scene of identity. The asymptotic metaphor has a similar limit, since it is fated to fall short of a 'true', a straight line, a perfection. These metaphors lead into the 'ontology of lack' perceived in Lacan and generally criticised.[9] Yet, Lacan also conceives of the subject through the metaphor of the sign, in such a way that his epistemological distinctions are not as black and white.

Freud, in the idea of 'stereotype plates', already hinted at the way in which knowledge is inevitably projection. The question becomes what other criterion can be used to evaluate, or even to approach the notion of, truth, when that of an independent reliability of the 'outside' can no longer be declared? In Freud's thought experiment, the nascent subject referred to *his own interior possibilities* for the 'first distinction': whether flight availed. For Lacan, too, a reconciliation in the subject moves from the inside out, from the states of unconscious desire and not from the projected objects of an external world. Where the latter is imposed – in therapy or philosophy – the result is disaster:

> the captation of the subject by the situation gives us the most general formula for madness, not only the madness that lies behind the walls of asylums, but also the madness that deafens the world with its sound and fury.
>
> (1977, 7)

The circumstances of the outside world depicted in the mirror produce that 'little reality' which is the subjective scene. For Lacan, it is not that psychoanalysis knows another reality; but only that it knows that the subject is connected to its desire as much as to the world, and must therefore approach its representations of the world in that 'knowledge'.

Lacan imagines he has done some violence to philosophy in having displaced the I, causing some anxiety for the Cartesian subject, the home of the philosophical. He asks: *Is what thinks in my place another 'I'?* A common philosophical interpretation of the Freudian unconscious imagines that there are two (or more) parts to the self.[10] However, where this leaves out the idea of repression, it does not render Freud. For it is not merely that the subject is divided, but that part of its psychical material is *held at a distance from consciousness*. And this is what Lacan sees as threatening to philosophy and science, the deputies of consciousness. If there were several 'I's, one could still know oneself in one or other of those guises. But: 'Who, then, is this other to whom I am more attached than to myself since, at the heart of my assent to my own identity it is still he who agitates me?' (1977, 172).

The goal of analysis for Lacan is for the subject to make conscious the discourse of the Other, the unconscious, in order to approximate reconciliation between the parts of itself. That goal is limited by definition, but this is the direction in which one finds pain relief. Where the distinction between 'I' and the Other is acute enough to be generating pain, then while there can be no synthesis, nevertheless a 'reconciliation' is needed. Reconciliation, he makes clear, does not produce a 'total personality' – and he sneers at various forms of psychotherapy which depict this as likely ('the moralistic tartufferies of our time').

On the ego–other axis of *Schéma L*, one may only understand oneself in relation to the small other, **a'**, but it is knowledge at the behest of the unconscious, and prompted by its desire. These object-images are that order of the psychical which Lacan designates the 'imaginary'. But the psychical is a compound of three orders, represented on the *Schéma L*. What moves unconscious desire is the order of the real; the subject's speech is the symbolic order. The relation between the 'imaginary' and the 'real' translates – or transforms – Freud's relation between the pressure and source of the instinct and its psychical representatives of object and aim. More generally, the psychical orders revise the Freudian principles, of the pleasure principle and the reality principle. Just as Freud's reality principle was an action internal to the mind, and not an event of the external world, so too Lacan's 'real' is no Kantian postulation of noumena. The real is a psychical order. And yet, Lacan insists 'there are no gaps in the real'. '[I]t is with the appearance of language that the dimension of truth emerges'; the symbolic is the dimension of truth, and in it occur the paradox, the alibi and the lie.

> By his discoveries, Freud brought within the circle of science the boundary between the object and being that seems to mark its outer limit.
>
> (1977, 175)

The science of the unconscious takes place in the field of 'the object and being', at a tension between the epistemic and the ontic. By this, psychoanalysis appears as the science whose object is the subject/object relation. Since this is the epistemic relation, then psychoanalysis is the science of knowledge as such. But, given the dedication of modern science to that which takes place 'on the side of the subject', i.e. the conscious point of view, it must be clear that as science, even in Lacan's own terms, psychoanalysis can be only partly faithful to it. Psychoanalytic knowledge will present its own difficulties for what is cherished as scientific knowledge.

To the extent that psychoanalysis knows, writes Lacan, then it recognises that the 'knot of imaginary servitude' must be undone by love, i.e. in the transference. Psychoanalysis must then also be the science of love. But love is not an altruistic effusion on his formulation – and the structural ambivalence of the relation to the other, even on the part of the good Samaritan, recommends mistrust of the reformer or the philanthropist.

The ontology Lacan proposes for the subject, as a consequence of the mirror relation, is not without other productive metaphors, including the model of the transferential relation itself.

> In the recourse of subject to subject that we preserve, psychoanalysis may accompany the patient to the ecstatic limit of the 'Thou art that', in which is revealed to him the cipher of his mortal destiny, but it is not in our mere power as practitioners to bring him to that point where the real journey begins.
>
> (1977, 7)

The distillation of an ethical relation which arises from psychoanalysis begins from when one understands the subject's representations and self-representations as displayed in the *méconnaissance* of the mirror. Before this, one cannot enter into a relationship with the other at all. For one is in relation only to oneself, in mortal narcissism.[11]

8 Being

This passion of the signifier now becomes a new dimension of the human condition in that it is not only man who speaks, but that in man and through man it speaks (*ça parle*), that his nature is woven by effects in which is to be found the structure of language, of which he becomes the material.

(Lacan, 1977, 284)

Through the metaphor of the mirror, Lacan transforms Freud's image of the instinct, as the relation of the subject to the world. The itinerary of the drive describes the symbolic circuitry of that relation, as does *Schéma L*. But Lacan does not take up Freud's three aspects of metapsychology in any straightforward sense. What Freud had as a contradiction between the psychical image and the psychical as energy, Lacan translates onto a semiotic field where images carry a 'charge' of meaning, relative to other images.[1]

There is an 'actual', made up of semiotic fragments and their relations which form in the unconscious – indeed *they form the unconscious* as the subject's history. In Lacan as in Freud, these constellations do not only produce meaning, they produce experience – hence the last section of the paper 'The agency of the letter in the unconscious' can address 'The letter, being and the other'. The mirror stage depicts an epistemology *and* an ontology. In Lacan's 'metapsychology', Freud's idea of the transference is no longer a mere feature of practice, but one of the four 'fundamental concepts', the others being the drive, the unconscious and repetition.

The drive is the animation of the Freudian instinct, and the mental threshold; it exists for Lacan, too, in part outside psychology, which is an order of signs. Its signs are described as the instantiation of energy in image, the fixing of the drive in a certain form being what signification is. These *instances* make up the present, and the circuit of that energy into signification is accomplished, and thereafter known, in the processes of metaphor and metonymy.[2]

'The agency of the letter in the unconscious, or reason since Freud' is an outline of the Lacanian view of the subject. The title reflects the audience of philosophy students, students of 'letters'. In this paper, Lacan links Freud with the history of philosophy – specifically of a concept of (which is to say, a desire for) reason – and also with the structuralist social sciences, especially linguistics. Lacan makes pedagogical use of these in a critique of humanist philosophy given in this paper and elsewhere.[3]

Lacan undertakes to tell us the 'meaning of the letter'. He argues structuralism offers an understanding of the unconscious through the algorithm of the sign (Figure 4). This pictures the sign, the basic unit of

$$\frac{S}{s}$$

Figure 4 Saussure's algorithm of the sign.
Source: Lacan, 1977, 149.

meaning, as a ratio: The S is the 'signifier', the word as written, the 'letter'; the *s* beneath the bar is the signified, the concept or given meaning of the moment for which S stands. But, rather than reading language 'vertically' so that every idea of an object is picked out by its own unique name, Saussurian linguistics understands meaning on the metaphor of a network of horizontal references. Lacan's inspired example is the diagram using two WC doors (Figure 5). Meaning arises in the difference between two identical signifieds – ordinary doors. There is so much meaning in these signs, indeed, that to walk through one rather than the other is a defining act. Lacan's example puts his audience in the thick of the 'network of the signifiers', by which meaning is pro-

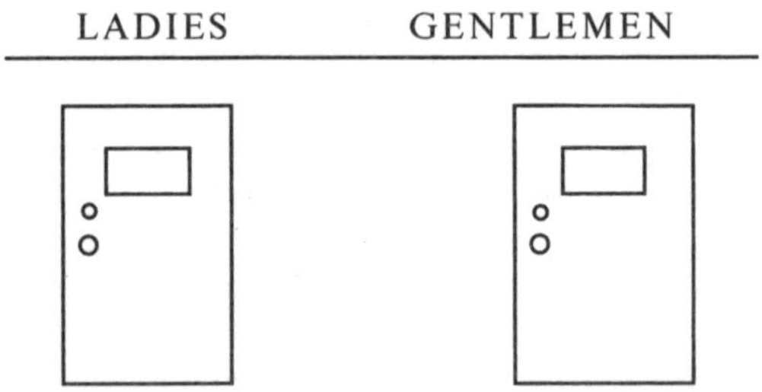

LADIES   GENTLEMEN

Figure 5 Lacan's illustrative example of meaning in Saussurian linguistics.
Source; Lacan, 1977, 151.

duced and even oppressively so, in this case of sexual differences. The sign is arbitrary as shown by the fact that different words attach to similar doors in reality; nevertheless, the distinction provokes social practices.

It is a habit of Anglophone readers to imagine language confined to the alphabetical sign. But if a network is constituted in the contrasts it recognises as different – at the simple level, the vocal, between *b*at and *c*at – differences can generate meaning at any level. For example, the difference between men and women comes to be seen in the penis in one order; thus, the penis is a signifier, Lacan's phallus. Semiotics observes orders that, from architecture to the body, operate as networks of meaning. Lacan is instrumental in extending this when he makes the subject itself a signifier. The subject becomes *a signifier for another subject*, the notion stressing the inherent relational character of identity (which was observed from the other side, in the mirror).

In arguing with a philosophical idea of the 'spirit', the humanist notion of the soul, Lacan resorts to the 'science of the sign' to resist more romantic views of the self. He depicts psychoanalytic concepts in terms of 'mathematical' formulae and structured symbols, the desire being to sidestep the temptation of an aesthetic subjectivity.

> Of course, as it is said, the letter killeth while the spirit giveth life. We can't help but agree ... but we should also like to know how the spirit could live without the letter. Even so, the pretensions of the spirit would remain unassailable if the letter had not shown us that it produces all the effects of truth in man without involving the spirit at all.
>
> It is none other than Freud who had this revelation, and he called his discovery the unconscious.
>
> (1977, 158)

It is a polemical exercise, to claim the unconscious is in the letter not the spirit, and its intent is to deprive the philosophical subject of self-satisfaction, the possibility that the *cogito* is the source of anything, original or originary. Instead, Lacan directs philosophy to that quadrature that represented the terms of subjectivity, and the 'self's radical ex-centricity to itself'.

The scandal in Freudian theory, Lacan writes, is not the salacious emphasis on sex, but how *intellectual* a conception of the self it is (but this, too, has its romance). According to Lacan, this is what Freud is mistrusted for among philosophers. 'The unconscious is neither primordial nor instinctual; what it knows about the elementary is no more than the elements of the signifier' (1977, 170). For Lacan, it is nothing more than a collection of signifiers seeking their signified in the moment of expression (which is the opposite of repression). Structured like a language, in that it is governed by processes of combination and selection just as in language, the unconscious is not a 'mystery', nor is it on the contrary to be despised – it is the terms of one's engagement with existence. The network of signifiers which is the unconscious is the tissue or *stuff* of life, 'the network in which, on occasion, something is caught'.

Indeed, the unconscious is represented elsewhere in Lacan as a hoop net, into which the object's image is sucked or breathed, through a narrow orifice. But it is what comes out of the net that interests the analyst – it is the discourse of the subject (1977b, 144). Freud's slogan, '*Wo es war, soll Ich werden*', is not a question of the ego (as it is usually translated) but of the subject. As Lacan translates it: Where it was, the *Ich* – that is, the *subject* – comes into existence. And there is only one method of knowing that one is there, 'where it was'; namely, 'to map the network' (1977b, 45). Lacan refers us to ch. 7 of 'The interpretation of dreams' to do so. The subject emerges from this 'network of signifiers', then, which is what the unconscious is.

The S/*s* algorithm can now stand for the subject, as 'the definition of the topography of the unconscious' (1977, 163). If it is read as depicting a psychical order rather than a natural language, the signifier S is that which the 'I' speaks, the bar is repression, and through its indirect pressure on consciousness, the unconscious is represented in the signified *s*. Freud himself expressed the idea when he wrote of the unconscious as having to 'borrow its voice'. Lacan makes cartographical use of Saussure's algorithm; mapping it onto the *Schéma L*, the broken line which joins the Subject of speech with the Other is intersected by the Saussurian bar, which is the reflective plane of the imaginary since it is the ego and its other relation which is blinding the subject to unconscious desire.[4]

In reading 'The interpretation of dreams' and other Freudian texts, Lacan finds an affinity between the Freudian protocol of condensation and displacement and the operation of the tropes of metaphor and metonymy. Since the subject is 'a network of significations', Lacan can borrow from structuralist Roman Jakobson a formulation of metaphor and metonymy as combination and substitution. This association he applies to the emissions – dreams, symptoms and speech – of the subject.

Metonymy, defined as word-to-word connection, and metaphor as one-word-for-another, leads Lacan to describe the dream rhetoric of displacement and condensation as metaphorical or metonymic processes, the linguistic insight making it explicitly an exercise of reading.

Through the concept of substitution, the choice of one word over another, condensation is understood as metaphor. Something comes to stand for something else, but in standing for it, the metaphorical term also covers it or disguises it. Thus, for Lacan, something is also 'occulted', repressed. Through this intuition, an association is developed between the trope of metaphor, the idea of condensation and the notion of repression and its failure in the symptom.

In a similar chain of argument, the concept of combination of words, the order of their connection, claims a relation between displacement and the trope of metonymy. Meaning is transferred onto something that is adjacent to it, either in time, space or other contiguity, and one associates the two terms in a metonymy by knowing their contingent relation in their occurrence in the world. The shifting of affect, and the structuring properties of proximity, reveal the trope of metonymy in displacement as a syntactical, and thereby a narrative, function.

Through these chains of association, a link is made between the linguistic categories, the notions of the 'letter' and the categories of psychoanalysis. By translating Freud into the language of structuralist linguistics, the protocols of the sign are transferred to the realm of the psychical.

> [i]f the symptom is a metaphor, it is not a metaphor to say so, any more than to say that man's desire is a metonymy. For the symptom *is* a metaphor whether one likes it or not, as desire *is* a metonymy, however funny people may find the idea.

> (1977, 175)

Now Lacan takes this circuit of associations further, into an ontological realm. *Metaphor – condensation – symptom – being*. The symptom is a metaphor, because the symptom is the replacement for the idea which has been repressed. It is the thing which both hides it, and expresses it for the unconscious. The symptom is a metaphor in the way earlier described – something standing for a repressed idea, as its sign – and 'it is not a metaphor to say so', for it is not merely by analogy that the unconscious has been found to be amenable to the sign.

The unconscious in Lacan's terms *is* structured like a language; language and the unconscious are related by more than metaphor. They are related by the representational character of subjectivity, of which language is an expression. Thus, it would be as true to assert, *language operates like the unconscious*, and in applying the categories of linguistic science to psychoanalysis, Lacan imagines he makes a scientific extension as much as he takes a literary licence.

At the other pole, Lacan's metonymic circuit closes on the lack of being (*manque-à-être*), the philosophical nothingness and the Freudian Thanatos. *Metonymy – displacement – desire – lack*. To describe desire as metonymy is to understand the endless displacement of objects in the place of the other, the identifications of the ego, as a necessary substitution. Indicated in the Oedipal surrender of the first love-object (the mother), the substitutions become the terms of the discussion, the expression of the successive present; they become the chain of signifiers which is the subject's speech, S. But the gaps between them show the truth, that they are not original love-objects, but substitutes. They form a chain, and through it passes a pulse of desire or (Lacan highlights the sado-masochistic metaphor) desire goes in chains. It is the symbolic order which harbours desire, because it is only in the idea of the letter that one can have the possibility of substitution (a symbol standing for its meaning).

Repetition is itself a sign of the inability of the image completely to capture the motion of psychical energy. It refers to the 'sliding of the chain of signifiers', which Lacan also calls desire, of the impulse, to fix a meaning to fix on an image, and of the failure to do so for more than the present moment.

The symptom is now a metaphor – that is, the rules of metaphor can be used to describe it. The action in the metaphor is not in either term, but in the fact that one does that for the other – this for Lacan expresses the relation between signifiers *per se*. It is in the differential that there is vivacity. And the 'genius of metaphor', the spark that flashes between the terms, Lacan sees as desire. Desire is metonymy, that is, the continuing movement onward through those signs which signify, in search of satisfaction.

> the slightest alteration in the relation between man and the signifier . . . changes the whole course of history by modifying the moorings that anchor his being.
>
> (1977, 174)

Being owes its form to the letter, and the letter works by the principle of repetition. This is what dictates the 'relation between man and the signifier'.[5] As ontology, this describes how experience takes the form its signifiers make possible, being the expression of the network of signs. Thus, to change the letter 'changes the whole course of history'.

The 'network' is an entity without a heart – the subject is nothing other than a history, and a material history since its signs are incorporated in the flesh. At the same time as the subject has no essence then, it is nevertheless highly specific to its circumstances. The peculiarity of each subject is preserved. If meanings are instances of being, then there is a sense in which, by definition, we do not mean, by the same signifier, the same sign. Private languages are not just a possibility but a necessity on Lacan's view. This creates the difficulty that transference bridges, and is also what makes it inappropriate for one ego to stand as the model for another.

In analysis, the attempt is made to understand the network of significations that cause malaise in one subject's being, what gives this being to the subject out of its unconscious; that is, to see the letter lodged in the body. Since the signs are flesh, to this extent they can be painful. For Lacan, human life is tied to the sign in a necessary and not contingent sense. Thus, if it is 'not a metaphor to say so', it is because symptom and metaphor arise from the same source, which is that (conceptual) medium in which the subject is composed of signs; the unconscious 'is structured like a language' and grammar is intimate to us.

Lacan has found in linguistics a figurative language with which to represent his psychoanalytic conceptions of the mechanism of experience. When he uses the algorithm of the sign to depict the subject, he is in earnest. The subject is another scientific object analysable as a sign structure. The potency (and paradox) of the Lacanian analysis (of psychology as much as of the subject) is produced in its own contrast to an empiricism that distinguishes a literal from the metaphoric, and thereby separates out the real from any representation of it.[6]

Metaphor is related to symptom, and connected to being in the sense that it is the sign, the letter, that fixes meaning, however provisionally. Metonymy is linked to desire, or the passage and the gap, thus to its lack, by nothing other than a movement which leaves a wake. In this attenuated metaphorising, Lacan arrives at the relation he sees between the letter, being and the other. To read the symptom as metaphor is not to believe that it is 'merely metaphoric'. *The symbolic has being; better, the symbolic produces being.* If there is a strength in Lacan's account it is that he makes it impossible to have a sign divorced from its material because the symptom is a material event, its pain has meaning and an experience of life is bound up in it.

This is the deduction of an epistemology and an ontology implied by the Lacanian signifier. While the sign is a relation, it is not necessarily one of truth. In fact, a representation is not true, rather, it *is*, it has being – this the cryptic figures of the dream show us. The tension in

Lacan's figure of the mirror, caught between truth and the simulacrum, is dissolved in the figure of the sign which, through its own figures of metaphor and metonymy, allow for looser relations, and principles of association other than replication.

9 Desire

A train arrives at a station. A little boy and a little girl, brother and sister, are seated in a compartment face to face next to the window through which the buildings along the station platform can be seen passing as the train pulls to a stop. 'Look', says the brother, 'we're at Ladies!'; 'Idiot!' replies his sister, 'Can't you see we're at Gentlemen'.
. . . For these children, Ladies and Gentlemen will be henceforth two countries towards which each of their souls will strive on divergent wings.

(Lacan, 1977, 152)

Lacan's view of desire and sexuality is joined to his general theory of subjectivity through the figure of the phallus. While the phallus appears to be unlike Freud's castration complex, there is a strong conceptual continuity between the Lacanian and the Freudian accounts.

The Lacanian version goes through metaphorical elaborations which make it at times unrecognisable. However, Lacan accepts from Freud the centrality of genital pleasure as a cause in the formation of character, and the foundation, therefore, of the psyche in the body. He presumes a psychical structure which grows out of the situation of the body and, more specifically, that the threat of castration is only believed in because of the *female* body, which is to say, he accepts the role Freud gives to sexual difference in forming the psyche. He accepts the bisexuality of the subject, and sources sexual orientation in the discovery of the two sexes, in the course of the socialising of the child.

The phallus is built faithfully out of the Freudian castration complex, and the prohibition on incest that this seeks to explain. The notion that this prohibition is the universal cultural threshold has not disappeared from Lacan's account, and is indeed the threshold of it. Lacan also makes the philosophical assumption, in common with Freud, that human being precedes sexual difference, and therefore can be considered more generally than the sex of the subject. On the basis of this assumption, it is no 'discovery', as he claims at the end of the paper on 'The signification of the phallus', that libido is singular and masculine – neither for Freudian theory nor for his own. That conclusion is built into the premises.[1] In general, because of all these assumptions, Lacan avoids none of the major commitments of the Freudian account.

The profound modulation in the Lacanian account is the move from historical actuality to structural necessity – the move from the developmental contingency of the castration complex to the symbolic imperative of the phallus. In effect, the concept of the phallus is the fulcrum of the Lacanian move from a science of the mind to a philosophy of the subject, which is to say, from empiricism to structuralism. The domain of the phallus is the symbolic, of which it is the sign:

> In Freudian doctrine, the phallus is not a phantasy, if by that we mean an imaginary effect. Nor is it as such an object (part-, internal, good, bad, etc.) in the sense that this term tends to accentuate the reality pertaining in a relation. It is even less the organ, penis or clitoris, that it symbolizes . . . For the phallus is a signifier . . . it is the signifier intended to designate as a whole the effects of the signified.
>
> (1977, 285)

The story of the phallus is a chain of associations. At the advent of the splitting of the subject, in the establishment of the mirror stage, a difference is created between the orders of the real and the imaginary. The difference between the real and the imaginary is that difference that arises between the appetite for satisfaction and the demand for love. Lacan presents desire, which arises at the Oedipus complex and establishes the symbolic order, as a sum that can be done in relation to these two earlier terms; as an operation of subtraction.

> Thus desire is neither the appetite for satisfaction, nor the demand for love, but the difference that results from the subtraction of the first from the second, the phenomenon of their splitting (*Spaltung*).
>
> (1977, 287)

Therefore: (*demand for love*) – (*appetite for satisfaction*) = *desire*, which in terms of the psychical orders gives: *imaginary* – *real* = *symbolic*. The virtue in this sum is its portrayal of the relation between the Lacanian orders, and specifically the connections between desire and signification. For signification is represented here as 'the phenomenon of their splitting'; and the symbolic retains that differential character.

In the play on mathematic terms, what began as an exercise in subtraction becomes one in division; the split subject is now the divided subject, otherwise known as a *ratio*. And the ratio, of course, is the algorithm of the sign: S/s. Returned to the linguistic formula of 'The agency of the letter', the bar now shows the thinking subject not only as divided but more specifically as *divided in its desire*. The bar becomes a representation of the phallus; and the phallus is recognised as a signifier.

> It can be said that this signifier is chosen because it is the most tangible element in the real of sexual copulation, and also the most symbolic in the literal (typographical) sense of the term, since it is equivalent there to the (logical) copula. It might also be said that, by virtue of its turgidity, it is the image of the vital flow as it is transmitted in generation.

> (*ibid.*)

The phallus at the same time becomes a transcendence in a dialectical mood: that which overcomes the imaginary and the real. A Hegelian account of self/other shows itself. The Hegelian–Freudian subject is explicitly formed here; the question of the demand for love is the question of the desire for recognition. *This is what links sexuality with identity in Lacan, on the same axis.*

It results, on Lacan's account, in identity's being lived through the love relation, through the erotic relation. This represents the thoeretical condensation of the master/slave dialectic onto the subject/object relation. Since the subject is divided, it has identity only in relation to the other (who or whatever that may be) – this was established in the mirror stage. Thus, in love one performs an operation which intimately concerns oneself. As evident from the mirror stage, Lacanian psychoanalysis can be read as a story about the securing of *consciousness*, which is neither a departure from Freud, nor yet from Hegel.

At the level of the question of identity, Lacan proposes that the subject has two imaginary wishes, in the recognition sought in the love relation:[2]

1 *I demand to be loved 'for myself'* – I do not want to be mistaken for my substitutions, my signifiers, my speech, which stand over 'me' and my desire. I want to be loved for that which is other than my attributes. I want to be recognised as other than what stands for me.
2 *I demand to be loved 'for mySelf'* – I want it recognised that I am divided. I want it accepted that I am alienated from my desire in repression.

This is what, in demand, pertains to identity. These translate in the sexual relation; I put my demand to the m/other in these terms, in asking for something of my own identity (which is the point of love):

1 *That I 'have' the phallus*, that I be given it, which is to say not to have the wound of castration, the split in the subject, even the 'vulva'. I desire not to be castrated, nor beaten by the rod of the father, subjected to the bar; I desire not to have desire repressed. This is the first link between the copula as erotic and as grammatical.

2 *That I 'be' the phallus*, that I be recognised not as the 'I' of my conscious discourse, nor as the unconscious desire, nor even to be recognised as both, but to be identified as their contest, or process; I desire to be seen for what I am, as a process which expresses itself in this alienated way. This requirement is symbolised in the bar-phallus; I desire to be accepted as barred, as split.

The demand for love directed to the mother will theoretically always be disappointed since the mother desires someone else *by law*. Whether the child is a boy or a girl, with or without a penis, the relation with the mother is not an appropriate love-match. The result of the phallic phase is the same for subjects of either sex; neither of the wishes for wholeness is satisfied.

These positions are not mutually exclusive, although logically inconsistent; they persist in the subject as expressions of its bisexuality. But they also characterise sexual difference. The wishes are carried into relations with the sexual partner. Heterosexuality can be described through them, since in the constitutionally bisexual subject – who can theoretically take up either position, and probably takes up both, to some extent, at least in relation to the mother – masculinity or femininity emerges as the predominant position. This is where anatomy is called on to play its part. It supports the symbolic drama at the level of physical form. While the phallus cannot be reduced to the penis (much less the clitoris), the phallus nevertheless has as its referent that organ – which returns us to Freud, to observe what problems stalled at the level of the physical, return at the symbolical.

What is the masculine position, and what is the feminine, out of these two wishes? In the masculine position, he demands of her that *she be the phallus for him*; that is, that she be whole and so contradict the father's threat of castration. Through this demand, he fantasises he can be whole, for she restores to him the possibility of not being repressed or alienated from his desire in signification. This wish will naturally be disappointed, setting up a 'centrifugal' force in masculine desire toward 'the other woman' as another opportunity for the proof. The figure of the phallic mother also represents the relief anticipated by the satisfaction of such a wish. The result is a link between masculinity and the pole of substitution, metonymy and so to desire (as lack).

But the feminine position demands of him that *he have the phallus*, and give it to her, to complete her lack, and restore the circumstance in which, although 'barred', she is whole. (This, too, is a fantasy of the phallic mother.) Since this he cannot give her, in response to this disappointment she is more likely to adopt a posture of repudiation of desire, that is, of 'frigidity'. The feminine position is brought closer to the pole of repression, metaphor and being.

In these two sexual positions, in the realm of the imaginary – it is a *méconnaissance*, in a 'fictional direction' – both wishes are, technically, disavowals of the painful condition of the split subject. This is why Lacan can say of being in love that it is 'in the dimension of making-a-mistake'. Because it is precisely in these wishes that one seeks confirmation of the *méconnaissance* in relation to the crisis of the threat of castration – 'what better way of assuring oneself, on the point on which one is mistaken, than to persuade the other of the truth of what one says!' (1977b, 133).

This *méconnaissance* is observed in clinical practice, in the following features, and his theorising of 'the phallus' allows Lacan to explain them: why the little girl feels herself to be deprived of the phallus by someone; why the mother is considered by both sexes for a time to have a phallus; why it is the discovery of her 'castration' that precipitates the 'Oedipal' crisis, and; why there should be a 'phallic' phase at all, i.e. one in which the clitoris and its pleasure is 'raised to the function of the phallus' (1977, 282).

Thus, while the masculine position reinforces the idea of castration, 'to be or not to be', the feminine reinforces the idea of penis envy, 'to have or not to have'; and they are both established as unconscious positions, as dramas of symbolism *in every subject*. The strength of Lacan's account over Freud's is that, whereas the more Freud could explain the masculine desire through the actual fear of castration, the less he could the feminine, Lacan can now also say 'what the woman wants', and through the same device. *The phallus explains both in one operation.*

> to put it in the simplest possible way, that for both partners in the relation, both the subject and the Other, it is not enough to be subjects of need, or objects of love, but that they must stand for the cause of desire.
>
> (1977, 287)

Now, this being an impossible demand, it returns the demand to the subject, as a demand on him for recognition of his essential *méconnais-sance*. 'This truth lies at the heart of all the distortions that have appeared in the field of psychoanalysis on the subject of the sexual life. It also constitutes the condition of the happiness of the subject' (*ibid.*). It illustrates 'how the sexual relation occupies this closed field of desire, in which it will play out its fate', and finally, will also explain why the transference, in also encroaching on this field, can intervene in the terms of being. *The cure is effected by love.*

To disguise the 'gap' in the subject, 'solely by recourse to the Other as reality' is 'fraudulent'. 'Man cannot aim at being whole . . . while ever the play of displacement and condensation to which he is doomed in the exercise of his functions marks his relation as a subject to the signifier.' *No one has the phallus*, and this is as much man's problem as woman's; every man is castrated. At that, the masculine and the feminine are joined, and the law of the father oppresses both in their imaginary relation, in their fiction.

The phallus is also therefore the name of sublimation. The law of the father is both something one must love (as Socrates argues in *The Laws*, one owes it to oneself to do so); but it is also against one, indifferent and even punitive. The subject itself is 'in an awful bind' – the super-ego is a persecutory formation, as Freud knew; and paranoia is our ontological agony. This, too, is 'not a metaphor to say so'.

Can one make the same criticism of Lacan that Freud makes against Jung, that in the figure of the phallus, something is being sublimated – thus, sublated – of the literal sexual aetiology into the abstraction of identity? While granting that Lacan's is a more cerebral and philosophically educated formula, is the phallus itself, in being abstracted, being sublimated from its role as a sexual denominator in the Oedipus complex? As the underpinning of the signifying system, it runs the risk of making the idealising move (which in Jung, describes instinctual energies as not sexual, but sacred), moving the theory away from the specificity of a sexual, bodily base. This 'theological' move forms the basis of Derrida's critique of Lacan.[3]

> The phallus is the privileged signifier of that mark in which the role of the logos is joined with the advent of desire.
>
> (1977, 287)

The effect of Lacan's notion of the phallus has been to recast 'the problem of femininity' for psychoanalysis and this has had effects also in feminist theory of sexual difference. In characterising sexual identity as a polarity imposed 'by law' on polymorphous perversity – enacted and enforced through anatomical differences – Lacan transfers the debate on sexuality from the biological, the natural and even the cultural to the order of the symbolic, the realm of law and logic.

In this realm, 'woman' is a sign, and it signifies an exclusion, 'not-man'. Thus, 'There is woman only as excluded by the nature of things, which is the nature of words' (Mitchell and Rose, 1982, 144). Freud's 'constitutional bisexuality' now refers to the symbolic possibility (and the real impossibility) of any subject being either masculine or feminine. But the subject itself, as an idealisation, is masculine – this is the consequence of the Freudian libido's being masculine, but is in fact more originally an effect of taking human being as *a priori* unsexed. For the same reason, the law is a 'paternal metaphor' – Lacan admits – and with the result that there is no feminine subject position. The feminine is only ever an idealisation, which is to say, an objectification, the subject's projection of its 'other'. But is Lacan, in claiming the law of the father, merely himself in the grip of the Oedipus complex, describing femininity as purely possible only as the cipher of the father's object of exchange?[4]

This leaves the subjectivity of those who find themselves 'on the side of the feminine', i.e. women, in foreign territory. A woman takes up her subjectivity as something foreign to her sexuality, since that can only be masculine, and she takes up her sexuality, also, as something foreign, since femininity is an *object* position not a subject position. This seems to be the distilled 'authority' of Lacan's *Encore* seminars.

And it follows from this rendering of the feminine as a purely projected '*objet petit a*', that there is nowhere 'else' where the feminine might be; that this 'other' merely records its opposition to 'self'. Put another way, 'feminine' is a legal term, found exclusively in the code of the law of the father. This theoretical consequence has predictably disturbed some feminists. Yet, as Jacqueline Rose points out, this is all predicated on a conviction Lacan himself stresses elsewhere, which is *the impossibility of the subject itself*. The unconscious guarantees that the subject is divided *ab initio*, and is never one identity. If there is no sexual relation, it is because there is no subject, and his object, too, is only the more visible fantasy.

In Lacan's formulation, anatomy is now, not destiny, but discourse (which may, nevertheless, amount to the same thing). There is no identity outside of discourse, which is to say, it is nothing other than a representation; 'identity', as a kind, belongs to the logical and not to the real. As such, human identity, sexual identity and logical identity are all subject to the arbitrary, differential paradox of the sign.

For a full appreciation of Lacan's pessimism, it is necessary to recall that the body itself is a sign. The subject does not have unmediated access to the 'real', even to that of his or her own body – experience is itself never a brute fact, but always a set of psychical representations; and even sensation is a sign. Yet Lacan is, strictly, following Freud here, however oblique the trail, because it was for Freud that consciousness was always a *mediation*, postulated as that state of the psychical in which the word-presentation was joined with the thing-presentation (the 'signifier' fixed – however briefly – on a 'signified').

These rhetorical consequences of the phallus suffer from the same weakness as the 'fictional' commitment of the mirror metaphor.[5] For, while the 'unified subject' is not logically possible, any more than 'fixed meaning' is, in the absolute terms its fantasy (psychosis) seeks, nevertheless the subject *does* fix itself at every moment in each of its projections. Arguably, this is the very evidence of subjectivity, of its process. Seen more positively, the constant translation of instinctual energy into psychical image is nothing other than the continuing process of expressing identity as a historical entity. Gayatri Spivak has put this well when she has said that it is just as much a matter of how the subject comes to be centred, as decentred (Brennan, 1989, 206). If Lacan's polemic has a fault, it is that it stresses the pole of collapse more than the pole of construction.

The way out of Lacan's net does not come through a critique of sexual difference (let alone of sexual politics) but through a critique of *discourse*. Lacan articulates the fantasy of sexual difference as 'embodied' in the phallus; in doing so, he has at least shown how *identity is our passion* – in the double sense of desire and suffering, and that the law of the father is the law of identity. The sanction, too, which he proposes – the lack of accomplishment of this desire, is undoubtedly shown as taken out of our flesh. But how does one represent the body in theory? One cannot, as other than a representation. This is a problem for psychology; it is the same problem for the psychology of the subject as for the philosophy of theory as such. Lacan's phallus becomes, at a certain point, ortho-authoritarian, seizing up in a kind of rage, caught in its net of signifiers as in a trap or cage. Lacan is profoundly ambivalent on this score; the net metaphor is after all his own (1977b, 144). As a Nietzschean master, he leads his disciples into the trap, and leaves them in it; *Lose me and find yourselves.*[6]

This may be fitting, since the position of the master (the father) is psychotic, trying to fix a meaning, when meaning cannot be fixed (arrested authority). Is it idle to note the surfacing of the Freudian–Lacanian conviction, tying logos to phallus, in the era of reason where, arguably, the subject, the masculine, the individual and technology coincide and intensify as violence? Perhaps the configuration occurs only now that one reads the history of kinship as the history of the exchange of women-objects – and reads *that* reading as being in the grip of the Oedipus complex, 'woman' appearing only as another *word* for object?

10 Cure

[Our patient] is impotent with his mistress, and, having taken it into his head to use his discoveries about the function of the potential third person in the couple, he suggests that she sleep with another man to see.

But if she remains in the place given her by the neurosis and if the analysis effects her in that position it is because of the agreement that no doubt she long ago made with the patient's desires, but still more with the unconscious postulates that were maintained by those desires.

And it will come as no surprise to learn that without stopping, even at night, she has this dream, which, freshly minted, she brings to our unfortunate patient.

She has a phallus, she feels its shape under her clothes, which does not prevent her from having a vagina as well, nor, of course, from wanting this phallus to enter it.

On hearing this, our patient is immediately restored to his virility and demonstrates this quite brilliantly to his partner.

What interpretation is indicated here?

(1977, 266–7)[1]

In analysis – through representation as screen memory, actual memory or dream – the patient comes to re-order his relation to past structures. Lacan tells us: 'The patient is not cured because he remembers; he remembers because he is cured' (1988, 13).

The task in analysis is then to recount the past as story, and in terms that link it to the present surroundings. But this is only possible because the text of experience is now opened to view; the censorship lifted. (The moment called 'fixated' is more properly a *preserved* moment, an image embalmed as desire itself.) This extends the idea that consciousness is the faculty of representing; in finding speech for the occluded image, the 'word-presentation' is united with the 'thing-presentation' – Lacan reads Freud's paper on the 'Unconscious'. What is pain, if it can be relieved by articulation? But the point is not that speech cures painful affect (despite its 'special powers'), it is that *making conscious allows representation, which is to say, release.*

> Can you see where this is all leading to? It leads, within Freud's own conception, to an idea that what is involved is a reading, a qualified and skilled translation of the cryptogram representing what the subject is conscious of at the moment – what am I going to say now? of himself? no, not only of himself – of himself and of everything else, that is to say of the whole of his system.
>
> *(ibid.)*

The task of interpretation is foreshadowed in the title to one of the 'Papers on technique', 'Remembering, repeating and working-through'. To remember is to establish a present distinct from the past – in repetition, since the unconscious is timeless, everything remains before the ordering imparted by time, in a conceptual 'pre-historic'. When Freud conceives of consciousness as a kind of sensing, he means to give it the nature of event, thus allowing for the 'making-present' and likewise its corollary, the 'making-past'. Working-through is the curious technique of analysis, in which the repetitions which impose themselves on the present as forms of resistance are interpreted.

The resistance is unconscious, and gives one of the best examples of what it is for an idea to be unconscious. The unconscious, writes Lacan, is 'what closes up again as soon as it has opened' (1977b, 143), and transference is its closing up, when 'the beauty is taken back behind the shutters' – but she is the one to whom the analyst's interpretation must speak. Transference, therefore, is 'a mode of access to what is hidden in the Unconscious'. '[T]he transference is both an obstacle to remembering and a making present of the closure of the unconscious, which is the act of missing the right meeting just at the right moment.'

An aspect of this unconsciousness remains obscure; Freud senses it as the instinct's pressure but, for Lacan, the same intuition is stated with another emphasis, as 'speech's incompatibility with desire'. If consciousness is the event of representing, and the unconscious a 'network of signifiers' waiting to be pressed into service, then that part of the psychical which is pure energy (which is vivacity, *pulsion*, drive) flows on and away. It cannot be said, not because it is secret, but because it is not symbolic (it is indeed 'real', according to Lacan's orders).

What interpretation is indicated here? In Lacan's story of the neurotic, an interpretation of a desire has been offered in the form of the mistress's dream. It is a successful interpretation, as evidenced by the fact that he is cured of his impotence. Thus, the therapeutic relation in the story is the one between the mistress and the neurotic, not between the analyst and the neurotic – and Lacan's intuition places the sexual relation itself in relation to a therapeutic and epistemological possibility. On his view of the transference, epistemology – and analysis – take the sexual relation as a prototype.

Interpretation answers the fiction of demand, the *méconnaissance* of love. The neurotic is a knowing man; he knows a thing or two about psychoanalysis, and attempts (as Freud predicts he will) to defend himself against the theory with the theory, to resist psychoanalysis by getting the analyst to confirm a diagnosis. But like Scheherazade, with an eye to her own survival, the mistress produces a dream that satisfies the neurotic, that answers the neurotic's desire at the place beyond demand. The mistress dreams for him and what she gives him is the avowal of desire. Her dream permits castration, even while it also bestows the phallus. It allows her to be in both the feminine and the masculine positions.

By that, it is almost as if she offers him a theoretical proposal: 'I understand your impossible desire, to have and not have, to be and not to be'. His impotence shows he is compulsively caught up in representing a desire whose satisfaction at one level would be contradicted at another. The symptom represents a division against oneself, the mark of unconscious conflict. But the mistress is able to answer the anxiety, not by affirming one or other side of the dichotomy – she shows him, as one subject to another, that *it is inevitable that one will be divided like that*.

It is inevitable that he will experience desire as impossible. As a matter of theory, her dream presents desire as a contradiction. Thus, the paradox of desire 'is not the privilege of the neurotic, it is rather that he takes the existence of paradox into account when confronting desire. This does not give him such a bad position in the order of human dignity, and does no honour to mediocre analysts ... who on this point do not achieve the same dignity', Lacan concludes (1977, 272).[2]

Lacan summarises the fault he sees in ego-psychology as an intellectual one: 'thus at best the present day analyst leaves his patient at the point of purely imaginary identification in which the hysteric remains captive'. An analysis that has found yet another fixation for the desire, another 'cure'. But this leaves the subject still in the cycle of appropriating objects to the demand; it leaves him in the chains of metonymy of desire. Instead, Lacan prescribes 'the freedom to avow one's desire', and it is 'what the subject tolerates least easily'. In refusing to satisfy in the register of demand, the analyst follows through a technique from elsewhere: interpreting resistance, rather than allowing it to perform its reality-giving function. 'Since no obstacle is put in the way of the subject's avowal of his desire, it is towards this avowal that he is directed, even shepherded.' A crisis must eventually ensue for the subject in the transference, as in the case of this neurotic, at the point where he can no longer escape the sense of *dejà vu*, or repetition.

Lacan complains elsewhere that there is no sexual relation; if too often the sexual relation is reduced to that of subject and object, women find themselves objectified for masculine desire in fact and in law. But if there is a tenderness in the teaching of the mistress to the neurotic, it is that she does not permit that reduction *even as* she offers herself as an object to his love.

Between the mistress and the neurotic, beyond the *content* of her interpretation, her act of submission in becoming his object allows the ambiguity in intersubjective relations to affect him, without reducing either of them to the unproblematic status of object or subject. As such, the terms of the experience of subjectivity can be made conscious; the ambivalence of the relation to the other is restored. The vignette shows the power of love as a relation between subject and subject, and demonstrates why, as a matter of theory, the cure *is* effected by love.

Where does that leave the patient for Lacan? *It leaves him without his symptom.* He is left in an anticlimactic environment, in a less glamorous place than the ensnarement at which the cure might have been thought to be effected, earlier in the ego-identifications of the analysis. It leaves him at the point at which it has lost its point. If the recognition that desire is divided has eased the pain – this is a cure 'by philosophy'. The hysteric suffers from ideas, and is also relieved by them.

If psychoanalysis is a philosophy, it also constitutes itself as therapeutic. It conceives of itself as an antidote – the corrective of consciousness. But there is a paradox at work in psychoanalysis – on the one hand, it is a recuperative effort for those qualities of existence which are left out, silenced, crushed or broken in the aggressive march of rationality. It is on the side of the unconscious. On the other, it seeks to colonise, to tame and domesticate the wilder sides of life for scientific and therapeutic ends. Psychoanalysis itself harbours ambivalence to which its churches, its heretics and feuds attest.[3]

In general, psychoanalysis challenges: is conceptual effort essentially directed at destroying chthonism, or at releasing it? As a stylistic problem, at least, this question has been with philosophy since Nietzsche. How far can reason collaborate with itself, and how far can it go in undoing itself before nothing can any longer be comprehended, which is to say, conceived? In the wake of anticlimax, *how is one to understand the possibility of cure?* In a hymn to Freud, Lacan expresses a metaphysical intent:

> Who, more fearlessly than this clinician, so firmly tied to mundane suffering, has questioned life as to its meaning, and not to say that is has none, which is a convenient way of washing one's hands of the whole business, but to say that it has only one meaning, that in which desire is borne by death.
>
> (1977, 277)[4]

Lacan resists negative theology – philosophical atheism of the existential kind – in the claim that to declare that life has no meaning is an act of surrender. Nevertheless, in holding to the idea of desire being borne by death, he proposes his structure of desire and lack as the ontology of psychoanalysis.

The provocation to analysis being the occurrence of pain, the question of the cure is not a mere palliative – nor is it a question that medicine, or psychology, has a lien on. As a condition of living, it falls to be negotiated in philosophy and theology. Lacan's pious tone puts psychoanalysis in that tradition of a 'search for wisdom', at one with philosophical and religious impulses. Can it, on the other hand, have avoided being enacted as a science, since that is now where we pray?

What other function than the religious grants reality? The contest over the real is an extraordinary, live conflict. Science is in this respect, and whatever else it is, continuous with the life-giving project of all ontologies, which are sacred to their constituencies. This requires that science itself be understood as a species of theology, instead of as a cure of it. The description of fact is the sacred writing of the contemporary world, and that world worships where things are taken literally. No greater compliment can be paid than to grant something this reality.

It is not that scientific discourse is wrong, nor is it deluded. It is not that there are no facts – but, on the contrary, that *facts are expressive of contemporary desire*. The objective tenor of the scientific discourse may be the voice of God, yet, says Lacan; 'The true formula of atheism is not *God is dead* . . . the true formula of atheism is *God is unconscious*' (1977b, 59). Which is to say, *science is not recognised as worship*, so real is the ontology produced. Surely the world of the older gods was as real to the Greeks? But it is precisely the animation that the desire lends its representation, while it is a living one, that renders the others mere effigies, obsolete, ash. One can no longer imagine thinking like that.

The extent to which we are unconscious of our gods makes the metaphor of theology when applied to science seem strange and, at the same time, germane. Psychoanalysis questions the manner by which its artefacts become real, and through the relation that represents desire, the relation between self and other. The issue becomes: *how is reality fashioned in representing it?* Even this distinction is a pathology, which is to say, it is symptomatic of a wish. It remains the empiricist wish for the real to be prior, independent, and separate from its garb, its lieutenant and its sign. Analysis can not eradicate this potent desire, but only make conscious its contradiction.

If psychoanalysis addresses the pain of the metaphysical condition, in life and in the session, as intrinsically treated in relation to another, then it does so as a demonstration of its theoretical task, to relate the subject to the world, the inside to the outside. Psychoanalysis earns its theoretical place in psychology/philosophy not so much for the quantity of knowledge it has assembled on the sexual relation – notwithstanding what it has to say on femininity, masculinity and the formation of those positions; fetishism, homosexuality, other perversions, hysteria and neuroses. What psychoanalysis is distinguished for is its comprehension of the theoretical distinction which upholds the endeavour of sex *and* science; its understanding of the subject–object distinction.

Psychoanalysis has theorised sexuality explicitly as the subject's relation to objects. Beginning from the Freudian theory of instincts and elaborated in the Lacanian mirror stage, the subject is represented as one who must reach beyond itself to the world through its desire. It is the action of the libido which brings the subject into connection with the world at all.

The primordial act of identity is a love relation, founded on an act of desire. The formative relation is thereby a sexual relation. This makes of knowledge a special kind of love; but it also makes of love an epistemological relation. The subject, on the psychoanalytic model, is found in its objects, found in the way its objects are experienced for the subject in its desire. On such a model, science is not distinguished from sex through the question of desire, because desire underlies both. The distinction between the subject and the object is determined in the act of desire, the horizon being perpetually revised as subject and object change through the action of desire. It is precisely this vision which allows psychosis to be defined as 'the disturbance of the libidinal relation to reality'. There is no foregone location of the object or the subject, *a priori*; that is, determined in the action of desire. Psychoanalysis, in analysing sexuality, goes beyond sexual proclivity to an act of identity; to identity as such.

But this meets an impediment in science itself. A discourse in science (including psychoanalysis) takes sexuality as its object, against a horizon of subject and object already fixed. The debts to its empirical base mean it can do no other, since empiricism requires that the subject be a fixed pole in order for the object to be visible across subjects, and repeatedly so across times and places. The objective horizon is established then *before the scientific observation is made*, by disqualifying, and thus settling, the question of the subject's identity in advance, through a fictional postulate of equivalence. Thereafter, any intrusion of subjectivity is a taint.

While a potent conceptual procedure, this also represents a desire; empiricism represents a specific relation of subject and object, and a specific erotics. And having fixed it in advance, what preclusions will it necessitate in that variable relation – what other relations between subject and object will it rule out, and other kinds of desire overcome? Particularly considering that its desire for the subject seems primarily to be *a priori* that the *subject not desire*. The ubiquitous desire of science – that there be a separation between subject and object and that the object carry the burden of desire – represents a wishfulfilment. Indeed, science fulfils this desire every day, when it works on that plane of the objective as though it were real, and with these facts as if they were its own.

The difficulty this poses is nowhere more clearly seen than in the discussions of psychoanalysis as itself a science. In the sense that the scientist, the theorist and even the philosopher, take it upon themselves to analyse the position of the object, then it will become a question of 'the analyst's desire'. Psychoanalysis complicates the view from the 'inside', but also that from the 'outside', in its enigma of the analyst who is witness, observer, scientist, collaborator, healer and agent in the reaction. And who also makes up part of the material world, including that exemplar of material, the body. That this material – the 'inside', the 'outside, 'self' and 'other' – is demanding, yielding, exigent and recalcitrant – demonstrates the rich philosophical territory where psychoanalysis takes place, and stakes a claim to comprehension.

What are the concepts that psychoanalysis has forged, and which today seem to fall to hand? *The unconscious, repression, instinct, sublimation, desire, analysis* . . . such depict the possibilities now, in conceiving of oneself. Why is this? The idea of the unconscious comes in the wake of consciousness, of its 'enlightenment'. And, the vociferation of rationality cannot but bring out the insistent 'irrational' – that which it excludes as mad, as corporeal, as mechanical or as occult.

Notes

1 BODY

1 The choice between the term 'mind' and that of 'psyche' has been a rhetorical one throughout this study. While the use of 'mind' emphasises the effects of the mind–body opposition, the notion of 'psyche' occasionally serves to avoid them. The question is similar to that of the difference between 'instinct' and 'drive', discussed later in this chapter.

2 Cf. Ellenberger on Darwinism and psychoanalysis (1970, 231), and Freud (1987).

3 The political metaphor is never far from Freud's thinking, in describing the censorship of the dream for example, or the ego as a constitutional monarch (in 'The ego and the id', Freud, 1923).

4 The relation is well described by Lacan in *The Four Fundamental Concepts of Psychoanalysis*. And in 'The mirror stage' Lacan observes that the 'I', once established, is 'that apparatus for which every instinctual thrust constitutes a danger' (1977, 5).

5 While not framed as a story of subjectivity, Freud's account does deal with the formation of character. This can be seen explicitly in the story of sexual development; for example, in the consequences of the anal phase which receives its own treatment in an essay, or in Freud's paper on creative writing and day dreaming, in which a mental defence from early in life becomes a way of life.

6 Of course, to characterise this as 'desire' is to draw in the Lacanian reading, which forms the bridge to contemporary philosophical interest. Critique of psychoanalysis as an ontology of lack begins from this point, since Freud's organism wants. It is no doubt possible alternatively to view that organism more positively as in symbiosis with its environment – this would change the ontology. But it does not invalidate a story told from the point of need, which is the commitment of psychoanalysis. Any story of mental life can be expected to account for a number of philosophical phenomena, including knowledge – to start from the position of need, rather than from the idea of the mind as a recording device, has epistemological consequences.

7 Cf. the style of medical examination of women in Freud's time, exploited in the dream of Irma. But cf. Lacan, who asks his fellow practitioners, 'Have you ever, for a single moment, the feeling that you are handling the clay of instinct?' (1977b, 126).

8 Cf. Freud, who outlines this development of the libido theory in 'Beyond the pleasure principle' (1920, 50–3).

9 Life as a very rare species of death ... to remark that life and death instincts amount to life as a detour to death is like depicting one thing of which the other is a relation. There is no life of itself, but only this relation to its negation, death, not-life. The dualism proposes a logic, rather than a state of affairs. Elsewhere in 'Beyond the pleasure principle', the logic is represented as presence/absence and even *fort-da*, the child's game which has captured imaginations – the whole book is a sustained fugue on oppositional logic, on Derrida's reading of it in 'To speculate on Freud' (in Derrida, 1987). The life/death story is one about opposition as such, and Derrida reads the whole of Freud's theory as a kind of allegory of metaphysical thinking and its limit; see also 'Différance' (Derrida, 1982).

10 Wittgenstein's reasons perhaps have to do with positivism and protecting subjective life from its influence.

11 The same may be said of the concept of 'Q' from the earlier 'Project for a scientific psychology' – I thank D. Coulter for bringing this to my attention in an unpublished paper of his own on transference.

12 Lacan refines on need and satisfaction along lines that follow Freud's closing remarks in this paper on the polarities of mental life. The biological becomes his symbolic order, and the economic becomes the imaginary – the real remains as such. Need, demand and desire are the attenuations owed to the real, the imaginary and the symbolic. But the bifurcation of existence into several orders is theoretically necessitated by the depiction of the mind as a 'field of negotiation' and creates for Lacan a virtual space ('*un peu de réalité*').

13 This assumption is addressed in work of Bachelard on scientific concepts – see, for example, *The Psychoanalysis of Fire* (1987, 1–6).

14 In this connection, Heidegger's (1977) reading of technology as a task of moral maturity comes to mind.

15 The investments that French theory has made in relation to Freud reflect several intellectual generations of working with psychoanalytic theory. Thus, concepts which to English-speaking philosophical readers now seem fresh and usable are not always so for Deleuze, Derrida and Foucault.

2 DREAMS

1 As an example of an intepretation of a dream using these principles, Freud offers us an analysis of a 'specimen dream', the dream of Irma (1900, 96–121). 'The interpretation of dreams' is full of examples, which is a necessary part of Freud's persuasion, given that quality of the dream to represent contingent and highly specific meanings.

2 As Derrida points out, Freud was grappling with this in the ideas of breaching that he draws on in the 'Project for a scientific psychology'. Derrida's analysis in 'Freud and the scene of writing' explores the conceptual movement of the breaching, through various metaphors of text and apparatus. See Derrida, 1978.

3 The question Deleuze poses for Hume's picture of the mind is germane

here. Deleuze identifies Hume's inquiry as, 'How does a collection become a system?'. See Deleuze, 1991, 22.

4 Ricoeur, in his reading of Aristotle on catharsis and plot, offers one such outline in considering the truth in poetry. See in particular section five of the first study of *The Rule of Metaphor* (Ricoeur, 1978, 35–43).

5 Wittgenstein's complex theoretical relation to Freud is beyond the scope of this discussion. However, it is worth at least noting that Wittgenstein himself felt affinities with Freudian theory, which he commented on, and even declared at one point that he was a Freudian. At the same time, his own preoccupations in philosophy in English did not always lead him down the paths of other European philosophers who were influenced by psychoanalysis. See, in general, Wittgenstein, 1979 and 1966.

3 LIFE

1 Cf. the metaphor as introduced in 'Three essays on the theory of sexuality' (Freud, 1905, 176); and also as it reappears in 'Civilization and its discontents' (1930, 69).

2 In the first essay, in a footnote, Freud notes that 'Psychoanalysis has found that all human beings are capable of making a homosexual object choice, and have in fact made one, in their unconscious' (1930, 145). Each of us is constituted bisexually, unconsciously, and the conscious behaviour one exhibits is the product of a history and of a construction. 'Thus, from the point of view of psychoanalysis, the exclusive interest felt by men for women' is what requires elucidation. Freud finds an account of that attraction that does not fall back on a notion of chemistry. He does not deny obvious chemical events, but he recognises that one must also tell a psychical story, since sex also happens at the level of ideas.

3 In considering the ills and oppression visited on human beings throughout history, Freud reminds us that pain, too, is a subjective matter, and that we cannot substitute our own sensibility for that of the people of the time. Thus, we cannot judge their pain (as, for example, intolerable). The observation illustrates how seriously Freud is committed to the lived reality of particular human being. For Freud, perhaps, there is no 'false consciousness' – only the unconscious.

4 One need look no further than the close of the essay on civilisation to see our own historical embodiment of the problem of evil. Writes Freud:

> I remember my own defensive attitude when the idea of an instinct of destruction first emerged in psychoanalytic literature . . . For 'little children do not like it' [Goethe] when there is talk of the inborn human inclination to 'badness', to aggressiveness and destructiveness, and so to cruelty as well. God has made them in the image of his own perfection; nobody wants to be reminded how hard it is to reconcile the undeniable existence of evil – despite the protestations of Christian Science – with His all-powerfulness or His all-goodness. The Devil would be the best way out as an excuse for God; in that way he would be playing the same part as an agent of economic discharge as *the Jew does in the world of the Aryan ideal*.
>
> (1930, 120, my emphasis)

5   Of all the slowly developed parts of analytic theory, the theory of the instincts is the one that has felt its way the most painfully forward. And yet that theory was so indispensable to the whole structure that something had to be put in its place. In what was at first my utter perplexity, I took as my starting point a saying of the poet-philosopher, Schiller, that 'hunger and love are what moves the world' [*Die Weltweisen*].

(1930, 117)

Then follows a useful summary of the evolution of the theory of instincts. Freud's account reminds us that anal eroticism is sacrificed to genital love, not extinguished in it – the place of violence in the prehistory of civilisation lives on as sado-masochism in that of the individual (as does the 'oceanic' feeling of the oral stage with which he begins the book).

4 SEX

1 Cf. Melanie Klein's far more detailed and ambivalent rendition of the psychical reality of the child (Klein, 1923).
2 For an authoritative account of Freud's theory of sexuality considered in the light of feminism, see Juliet Mitchell's *Psychoanalysis and Feminism* (1974); see also her introduction to *Feminine Sexuality: Jacques Lacan and the Ecole Freudienne* (Mitchell and Rose, 1982).
3 Feminist evaluations of Freud and Lacan have often led the way in theoretical study of psychoanalysis in English: a selection might include Brennan (1989); Feldstein and Roof (1989); Felman (1987); Gallop (1985); Grosz (1990); de Lauretis (1984); Mitchell (1974); Mitchell and Rose (1982); Ragland-Sullivan (1986). Seminal French feminist readings include Irigaray (1985), Kofman (1985), and the work of Julia Kristeva – for example, Kristeva (1982).
4 This set-up is precarious; at the same time as the boy is 'in love with' the mother he is also 'in love with' the father, who also satisfies need and provides pleasure. The other side to the Oedipus complex is the resolution of feelings for the father. Usually less visible, the homosexual aim in the Oedipus complex plays some part in its accomplishment, since, if the boy didn't also love the Law in the figure of the father, his submission to it might not come about.
5 Cf. Irigaray's analysis in 'The blind spot of an old dream of symmetry' (Irigaray, 1985, 11–129).
6 Freud settles a few scores with 'the feminists' and others:

For the ladies, whenever some comparison seemed to turn out unfavourable to their sex, were able to utter a suspicion that we, the male analysts, had been unable to overcome certain deeply-rooted prejudices against what was feminine, and that this was being paid for in the partiality of our researches. We, on the other hand, standing on the ground of bisexuality, had no difficulty in avoiding impoliteness. We had only to say: 'This doesn't apply to you. You're the exception; on this point you're more masculine than feminine'.

(1933, 116–17)

– a response, despite the disclaimer, of well-aimed impertinence.

7 Indeed, there may be in femininity, as in all 'deviant sexualities', less of an investment in the Law and, were morality and justice defined as comformity to a social will, then it might follow that those who do not receive such a social benefit may not uphold that will.

8 Irigaray argues that the feminine is naturally a riddle for Freud, since libido is always postulated as masculine in psychoanalytic theory, and sex is seen as a masculine event. Further, she argues that this reflects a *metaphysical* commitment, that there be only one kind of desire (masculine) and its negation, which is feminine.

5 LOVE

1 Those of the *Papers on Technique* that refer directly to the question of transference are 'The dynamics of transference', 'Remembering repeating and working through' and 'Observations on transference-love'. But what is technique? Part of the justification for Freud's silence on the art of analysis arises from the demands of the technique itself, he reports. For if the patient finds out too much about the method, which is designed to circumvent unconscious resistances, those resistances will use that very understanding for that end, thus prolonging the treatment to a tedious extent.

2 This raises the question: what model of human relations and healing does this imply? in it, one subject offers him or herself up as a lure or even as a sacrificial love-object to another. Freud makes free use of metaphors of battle and struggle, the wrestle with the demon, etc., to depict the effect sought as cure, i.e. the very thing which unconscious aims lack: an 'exposure to reality'. It is such exposure which produces the modification and therefore the 'progress' of sublimation, change and 'maturity'. But the question remains: *who is it* – analyst or patient – who is sacrificed in this process?

3 Cf. the discussion in Laplanche and Pontalis (1986) of Freud's paper, 'A child is being beaten' (1919, 177).

4 Cf. Freud's reflections on the effects of trauma, in, for example, 'Beyond the pleasure principle' (1920, 12) and in 'Introduction to psycho-analysis and the war neuroses' (1919, 205). The prestige of psychoanalysis was improved appreciably by its ability to describe the aetiology of war neuroses following the 1914–18 war.

5 Cf. Freud's comments in the 'New introductory lectures' on the serious and chronic nature of neurosis, and how long and laborious is its cure.

6 LANGUAGE

1 Cf. Derrida in 'Freud and the scene of writing' (1978), where he argues that deconstruction is not a psychoanalysis of philosophy. On the other hand, cf. Bachelard, whose foreword to *The Psychoanalysis of Fire* (1987) provides for the psychoanalysis of scientific concepts.

2 The following remarks of Freud's on scientific theory seem prophetic in the light of some of his French readers: Lacan, Foucault, Deleuze, Derrida. As with the remarks on the transference, these remarks occur as prefaces, or

introductory remarks on methodology, yet their implications are integral to understanding the influence of psychoanalytic theory. They make directions taken in hindsight more explicable; they establish conceptual affinities between Freud, structuralism and post-structuralism.

3 Cf. Derrida's essay, 'To speculate on "Freud"' (in Derrida, 1987), especially p. 265.

4 Freud goes on to say of biology that 'We may expect it to give us the most surprising information and we cannot guess what answers it will return in a few dozen years to the questions we have put to it' (1920, 60). Which nevertheless indicates his respect for that particular figurative possibility.

5 Our profound physical metaphors have been in the discourse since Aristotle, and have continued to be reorganised under pressure of observation. Cf., for example, Heidegger's discussion on cause in 'The question concerning technology', in Heidegger (1977, 313–18).

6 'I am going to ask you seriously, by the way, whether I may use the name metapsychology for my psychology that leads behind consciousness' – letter to Fliess, 10 March 1898 (Masson, 1985, 301).

7 Freud proposes these as 'the consummation of psychoanalytic research' (1915, 181).

8 'New introductory lectures' (1933, 32), where Freud uses the analogy of the contents of the core of the earth – he distinguishes between the plausible hypothesis of molten rock, which may not be able to be observed directly, and the fanciful suggestion that it is made up of strawberry jam (a 'product of human cookery').

9 In this fable, Freud locates the foundational energy of the psyche as being located in the id, distributed through the system, and used 'against itself' in the way he foreshadowed in 'The unconscious'. What marks the difference between the conscious and the unconscious is related to the frank love relation between the ego and the id, or the fate of object cathexes with which the ego manipulates the id, harnessing its force. The super-ego is perhaps the best example of that kind of harness, for in the super-ego, external love-objects which the id had cathected, in the figure of the mother and father, are introjected – the ego 'makes like' those figures in order to attract the love of the id (i.e. to attract the energy of the id to itself).

10 'As a young man I knew no longing other than for philosophical knowledge, and now I am about to fulfill it as I move from medicine to psychology', Freud confides to Fliess in 1896 (Masson, 1985, 180). Derrida makes an argument of Freud's conscious relations to philosophy in 'To Speculate on "Freud"', cited above. The 'significant passage' is found in *The Psychopathology of Everyday Life*, and is echoed in other statements on the relation between science, philosophy and religion. Cf. 'New introductory lecture' XXXV (in Freud, 1933).

11 This becomes significant on Lacan's account of the Oedipus complex, where the establishment of the unconscious is also the condition of language, in effect the hypothesis that one can only have the idea of language when one has learned to substitute for the first (literal) object.

12 She 'suffers from reminiscences'. But the account seems awkward in Freud, and is more fluent in Lacan since he moves into the language of linguistics and talks in terms of signification. When Lacan describes the unconscious,

then, as a chain of signifiers, he imagines them waiting to be joined with the signified in an act of perception.

7 KNOWLEDGE

1 Cf. Roland Barthes' structuralist discussions of language – the phrase 'institutionalised subjectivity' is used, for example, in the essay 'Authors and writers' in Barthes (1972).

2 This dissatisfaction he expresses everywhere; for example, cf. (1977, 226–32).

3 Cf. Lacan's analysis of the masculine subject in relation to the feminine in 'A love letter' (Mitchell and Rose, 1982).

4 That is, as the plane of the imaginary. The symbolic, represented in other depictions as the line between 'I' and the unconscious 'structured like a language', is elsewhere identified as the 'bar' in the Saussurian algorithm.

5 Note also: 'The dehiscence of the subject' and 'the specific prematurity of birth'. Through the image, the self can complete itself, and only through the other can the self complete itself. It seems immediately to engage us with a formulation of self and other.

6 The baby's 'flutter of jubilant activity' evokes Aristotle's intuition, expressed in the *Poetics*, that the pleasure of learning is natural to humanity, however small the capacity for it.

7 The death instinct, through the concept of 'aggressivity', has rejoined Hegel: the other is a danger to the self, it being necessary to complete self-identity at the same time as feared for this very power over one's identity.

8 Ragland-Sullivan, in her exhaustive exposition of Lacan, notes that the mirror stage is an epistemology (Ragland-Sullivan, 1986, 89–93). Cf. also Grosz's outline of the mirror stage in her feminist discussion of Lacan (1990, 31–49).

9 Cf. Derrida's critique of Lacan's formulation, that it represents a negative theology (in 'Le facteur de la vérité', in Derrida, 1987, pp. 411–96); Deleuze's view of psychoanalysis in *Anti-Oedipus* (Deleuze and Guattari, 1983) and elsewhere.

10 Cf. Donald Davidson's essay in Wollheim and Hopkins (1982).

11 Lacan criticises existentialism as somehow being caught in a trap of its own devising. Between the virtual reality and that which it stands for is a 'false truth' – the claim made against philosophy is that its knowledge is precisely a *méconnaissance*. His immediate engagement is with existentialism and 'philosophies of consciousness' that claim confidence in their knowledge. For example, the critique sketched of existentialism at (1977, 6): Lacan makes the association between German idealism and existential philosophies, when he puts them in the same sentence, in 'existentialism must be judged by the explanations it gives of the subjective impasses which have resulted from it'. According to Lacan, the problem for a contemporary philosophy of 'Being and Nothingness' – a reference to Sartre – is that it grasps the impasse of the subject only from the position of consciousness, and as such is credulous as to the projections of the ego. Whereas, 'We are not regarding the ego as centred on the perceptual-consciousness system', and, starting from the function of *méconnaissance* that 'characterises the

Notes 109

ego in all its structures', come to understand the ego and its projections as signs, as representation. No doubt, anglophone empiricism commits the same 'intellectual fault' in Lacan's view when it takes its projections for 'objective facts'. In short, the failing of philosophy is that it mistakes the imaginary for the real.

8 BEING

1 The term is elaborated and given a different, specific meaning by Julia Kristeva (Kristeva, 1982).
2 In the mirror stage, the subject is accumulating libidinally-invested images that will become the signifiers of the symbolic. But the ability to recognise that one substitutes for another in the regulated fashion of a network, that process of definition, is the intellectual accomplishment of the Oedipus complex. Before that, the imaginary images are more labile, they do not fix firmly enough to have public meaning in the manner of the symbolic. The realising of the algorithm at a given moment excludes other ambiguities, which represent ambivalences.
3 'Finally, if I am to rouse you to indignation over the fact that, after so many centuries of religious hypocrisy and philosophical bravado, nothing has yet been validly articulated as to what links metaphor to the question of being and metonymy to its lack, there must be an object there to answer to that indignation both as its instigator and its victim: that object is humanistic man and the credit, hopelessly affirmed, which he has drawn over his intentions' (Lacan, 1977, 175). Lacan accuses philosophy of humanism, the philosophy of the ego, as outlined in my previous chapter.
4 Lacan draws out metonymy and metaphor as algorithms in this fashion:

> This two-sided mystery is linked to the fact that the truth can be evoked only in that dimension of alibi in which all 'realism' in creative works takes its virtue from metonymy; it is likewise linked to this other fact that we accede to meaning only through the double twist of metaphor when we have the one and only key: the S and the *s* of the Saussurian algorithm are not on the same level, and man only deludes himself when he believes his true place is at their axis, which is nowhere.
> *Was* nowhere, that is, until Freud discovered it; for if what Freud discovered isn't that, it isn't anything.
>
> (1977, 166)

But cf. Derrida's critique of the Saussurian opposition of signified and signifier in, for example, *Of Grammatology* (Derrida, 1976, 27).
5 Lacan's account has the merit that it may allow for radical cultural differences, something Freud's sociology seems less able to do; in cultures where different signifiers operate, different practices – different being – would result.
6 If psychoanalysis is, then, a 'revolution in knowledge', it is this reversal to which it refers. But cf. Derrida's diagnosis of structuralism in *Of Grammatology*, where he notes 'everything that for at least some twenty centuries tended toward and finally succeeded in being gathered under the name of

language is beginning to let itself be transferred to, or at least summarised under, the name of writing' (1976, 6).

9 DESIRE

1 Cf. Irigaray, 'Così Fan Tutti' in *This Sex Which Is Not One* (1985b).
2 Cf.:

> the establishment of the subject by the signifier . . . explains the *Spaltung* in the subject and the movement of intervention in which that 'splitting' is completed.
> Namely:
> (1) that the subject designates his being only by barring everything he signifies, as it appears in the fact that he wants to be loved for himself, a mirage that cannot be dismissed as merely grammatical (since it abolishes discourse);
> (2) that the living part of that being in the *urverdrängt* (primally repressed) finds its signifier by receiving the mark of the *Verdrängung* (repression) of the phallus (by virtue of which the unconscious is language).
>
> (Lacan, 1977, 288)

3 Cf. 'Le facteur de la vérité' in Derrida (1987). Lacan's analysis of sexual difference makes use of accounts of the relation between representation and the real which rule out resort to the idea of an 'outside' of the problem, in which woman can be found. As Rose (1986) points out, that notion would render women outside language and history, ignoring the rhetorical effects of linking symbolisation to the body. It avoids the question that Lacan has put. Conversely, to argue that this reflects the androcentrism of culture condemns women to history and language. The problem has therefore moved to the order of oppositional logic. Derrida proposes the phallus to be a piece of negative theology – not as androcentrism, but as phallogocentrism, and argues the phallus is disingenuous in presenting itself as 'the signifier of the signifier'; i.e. it performs the same intellectual move as Hegelianism in general. Derrida thus identifies in Lacan a 'first principle' of a metaphysical kind. Cf. Lacan's own reference to the *Aufhebung* (1977, 288).
4 Cf. in general J. Rose's excellent discussion of the position in (Mitchell and Rose, 1982, 27–57). Rose quotes Safouan on the particular point (1982, 39).
5 The phallus is a metaphor for what can be known, and despite its ambivalence, its emptiness, represents the Law. When Lacan explores the notion of feminine *jouissance* in the *Encore* Seminar it is an afterthought; *jouissance* does not capture *différance* or excess. Thus, while diagnosing sexual (in)difference, it is not clear that the phallus avoids it. Is it really satisfactory to declare the theory to have been on the side of the mystic? (Mitchell and Rose, 1982, 147). Is the phallus in the service of excess; or does its veiledness belong to its inversion of positive terms?
6 The paradox is that this seems to have produced, more often than not, a blind discipleship – cf. Lacan's various biographers, who record him as shaman or charlatan: Schneiderman (1983), Clément (1983), Borch-Jacobsen (1991).

10 CURE

1 In indicating the direction of the treatment, Lacan offers these instructions:

(1) that speech is all-powerful in the treatment, that it possesses special powers;

(2) that, according to the analytic rule, the analyst is a long way from directing the subject towards 'full' speech, or towards a coherent discourse, but that the analyst leaves the subject free to try it;

(3) that this freedom is what the subject tolerates least easily;

(4) that demand is properly that which is placed in parentheses in the analysis, since the analyst is excluded from satisfying any of the patient's demands;

(5) that since no obstacle is put in the way of the subject's avowal of his desire, it is towards this avowal that he is directed, even shepherded;

(6) that his resistance to this avowal can, in the last analysis, only be the result of the incompatibility between desire and speech.

(1977, 275).

2 If Lacan had fallen for the ruse and had declared his patient to be a repressed homosexual, as he tells us he demanded, then he would have done what he accuses the ego-psychologist of doing – falling for the ego, engaged with the imaginary demand rather than with the desire beyond it, leaving the patient with an artifical fix. *Which may have served*, for better or worse; only, like religion, such a cure shares the features of psychosis, as Lacan defines that. It would almost certainly have resulted in the end of the relationship with the mistress; but this exists, as Lacan cannily points out, to satisfy something, a transaction between two unconsciouses, which presumably leaves each in debt to the other in their 'unconscious postulates'.

3 Cf. in this connection Foucault's important analyses of these institutions in *Madness and Civilization*, and *The Birth of the Clinic*.

4 Freud himself raises the problem of the cure in the discussion of 'Analysis terminable and interminable' (1937). There he reflects on whether the aim of analysis could really be to rid the patient of all neurotic potential, or rather, whether treatment should address itself to the present symptoms alone, and 'let sleeping dogs lie'.

Bibliography

Abraham, Nicolas and Torok, Maria (1994) *The Shell and the Kernel: Renewals of Psychoanalysis*, vol. 1, Nicholas T. Rand (ed. and trans.), Chicago: University of Chicago Press.

Bachelard, Gaston (1987) *The Psychoanalysis of Fire*, Alan Ross (trans.), London: Quartet.

Barthes, Roland (1972) *Critical Essays*, Richard Howard (trans.), Evanston: North-Western University Press.

Benjamin, Andrew (1993) *The Plural Event*, London: Routledge.

Benjamin, Jessica (1988) *The Bonds of Love: Psychoanalysis, Feminism, and the Problem of Domination*, New York: Pantheon.

Bernheimer, Charles and Kahane, Claire (eds) (1985) *In Dora's Case: Freud – Hysteria – Feminism*, New York: Columbia University Press.

Bersani, Leo (1986) *The Freudian Body: Psychoanalysis and Art*, New York: Columbia University Press.

Borch-Jacobsen, Mikkel (1991) *Lacan: The Absolute Master*, Douglas Brick (trans.), Stanford: Stanford University Press.

Brennan, Teresa (1993) *History After Lacan*, London: Routledge.

—— (1989) *Between Feminism and Psychoanalysis*, London: Routledge.

Cavell, Stanley (1987) 'Freud and philosophy: a fragment', *Critical Inquiry*, 13(2): 386–93.

Cixous, Hélène (1975) 'Fiction and its phantoms: a reading of Freud's Das Heimliche (The Uncanny)', *New Literary History*, 7: 525.

Clément, Catherine (1983) *The Lives and Legends of Jacques Lacan*, Arthur Goldhammer (trans.), New York: Columbia University Press.

David-Ménard, Monique (1989) *Hysteria from Freud to Lacan: Body and Language in Psychoanalysis*, Catherine Porter (trans.), Ithaca: Cornell University Press.

Deleuze, Gilles (1991) *Empiricism and Subjectivity*, Constantin Boundas (trans.), New York: Columbia University Press.

Deleuze, Gilles and Guattari, Félix (1983) *Anti-Oedipus: Capitalism and Schizophrenia*, Robert Hurley, Mark Seem and Helen R. Lane (trans.), Minneapolis: University of Minnesota Press.

Derrida, Jacques (1987) *The Postcard*, Alan Bass (trans.), Chicago: University of Chicago Press.

—— (1982) *Margins of Philosophy*, Alan Bass (trans.), Chicago: University of Chicago Press.

—— (1981) *Dissemination*, Barbara Johnson (trans.), Chicago: University of Chicago Press.

—— (1978) *Writing and Difference*, Alan Bass (trans.), Chicago: University of Chicago Press.

—— (1976) *Of Grammatology*, Gayatri Spivak (trans.), Baltimore: Johns Hopkins University Press.

Edel, Leon (1984) 'Transference: the biographer's dilemma', *Biography*, 7(4): 283–91.

Ellenberger, Henri (1970) *The Discovery of the Unconscious*, New York: Basic Books.

Feldstein, Richard and Roof, Judith (eds) (1989) *Feminism and Psychoanalysis*, Ithaca: Cornell University Press.

Felman, Shoshana (1987) *Jacques Lacan and the Adventure of Insight*, Cambridge, Mass.: Harvard University Press.

Foucault, Michel (1984) *The History of Sexuality: An Introduction*, Harmondsworth: Peregrine.

—— (1973) *Madness and Civilization*, Richard Howard (trans.), New York: Vintage.

—— (1973b) *The Birth of the Clinic*, A.M. Sheridan Smith (trans.), London: Tavistock.

—— (1972) *The Archaeology of Knowledge*, A.M. Sheridan Smith (trans.), New York: Pantheon.

Freud, Sigmund (1987) *A Phylogenetic Fantasy*, Ilse Grubrich-Simitis (ed.), A. and P. Hoffer (trans.), Cambridge, Mass.: Belknap/Harvard.

—— (1962–75) *Standard Edition*, James Strachey (ed.), London: Hogarth Press.

—— (1950) 'Project for a scientific psychology', in J. Strachey (ed.), *Standard Edition*, vol. 1, 281.

—— (1937) 'Analysis terminable and interminable', in J. Strachey (ed.), *Standard Edition*, vol. 23, 209.

—— (1935) 'An autobiographical study', in J. Strachey (ed.), *Standard Edition*, vol. 20, 3.

—— (1933) 'New introductory lectures', in J. Strachey (ed.), *Standard Edition*, vol. 22, 1.

—— (1931) 'Female sexuality', in J. Strachey (ed.), *Standard Edition*, vol. 21, 215.

—— (1930) 'Civilization and its discontents', in J. Strachey (ed.), *Standard Edition*, vol. 21, 57.

—— (1927) 'Fetishism', in J. Strachey (ed.), *Standard Edition*, vol. 21, 149.

—— (1925) 'Some psychical consequences of the anatomical distinction between the sexes', in J. Strachey (ed.), *Standard Edition*, vol. 19, 248.

—— (1925b) 'A note upon the "Mystic Writing-Pad"', in J. Strachey (ed.), *Standard Edition*, vol. 19, 227.

—— (1924) 'The dissolution of the Oedipus complex', in J. Strachey (ed.), *Standard Edition*, vol. 19, 173.

—— (1923) 'The ego and the id', in J. Strachey (ed.), *Standard Edition*, vol. 19, 1.

—— (1920) 'Beyond the pleasure principle', in J. Strachey (ed.), *Standard Edition*, vol. 18, 7.

—— (1919) 'A child is being beaten', in J. Strachey (ed.), *Standard Edition*, vol. 17, 177.

—— (1919b) 'The uncanny', in J. Strachey (ed.), *Standard Edition*, vol. 17, 217.

—— (1915) 'Papers on metapsychology' (including 'Instincts and their vicissitudes', 'Repression', 'The unconscious'), in J. Strachey (ed.), *Standard Edition*, vol. 14, 105.

—— (1914) 'On the history of the psychoanalytic movement', in J. Strachey (ed.), *Standard Edition*, vol. 14, 3.

—— (1914b) 'Papers on technique', in J. Strachey (ed.), *Standard Edition*, vol. 12, 85.

—— (1910) 'Leonardo da Vinci and a memory of his childhood', in J. Strachey (ed.), *Standard Edition*, vol. 11, 130.

—— (1905) 'Three essays on the theory of sexuality', in J. Strachey (ed.), *Standard Edition*, vol. 7, 123.

—— (1905b) 'Jokes and their relation to the unconscious', in J. Strachey (ed.), *Standard Edition*, vol. 8.

—— (1901) 'The psychopathology of everyday life', in J. Strachey (ed.), *Standard Edition*, vol. 6.

—— (1900) 'The interpretation of dreams', in J. Strachey (ed.), *Standard Edition*, vols 4 and 5.

Gallop, Jane (1985) *Reading Lacan*, Ithaca: Cornell University Press.

—— (1984) 'Lacan and literature: a case for transference', *Poetics*, 13: 301–8.

Gay, Peter (1988) *Freud: A Life for Our Time*, New York: Norton.

Grosz, Elizabeth (1990) *Jacques Lacan: A Feminist Introduction*, Sydney: Allen & Unwin.

—— (1990b) 'A note on essentialism and difference', in Sneja Gunew (ed.), *Feminist Knowledge: Critique and Construct*, London: Routledge & Kegan Paul.

—— (1989) *Sexual Subversions: Three French Feminists*, Sydney: Allen & Unwin.

Heidegger, Martin (1977) *Basic Writings*, David Farrell Krell (ed.), New York: Harper Collins.

Irigaray, Luce (1985) 'The blind spot of an old dream of symmetry', in *Speculum of the Other Woman*, Gillian C. Gill (trans.), Ithaca: Cornell University Press.

—— (1985b) 'Così Fan Tutti', in *This Sex Which Is Not One*, Catherine Porter (trans.), Ithaca: Cornell University Press.

Johnson, Barbara (1977) 'The frame of reference: Poe, Lacan, Derrida', *Yale French Studies*, 55/56.

Jones, Ernest (1961) *The Life and Work of Sigmund Freud*, Lionel Trilling and Steven Marcus abridged in one volume (three volumes 1953–7), New York: Basic Books.

—— (1959) *Free Associations: Memories of a Psycho-analyst*, New York: Basic Books.

—— (1956) *Sigmund Freud: Four Centenary Addresses*, New York: Basic Books.

Kerrigan, William and Smith, Joseph (1986) *Pragmatism's Freud*, Baltimore: Johns Hopkins University Press.

Klein, Melanie (1923) *Papers on Psychoanalysis*, London: Hogarth Press.

Kofman, Sarah (1985) *The Enigma of Woman*, Ithaca: Cornell University Press.

Kristeva, Julia (1982) *Powers of Horror: An Essay on Abjection*, Leon Roudiez (trans.), New York: Columbia University Press.

—— (1980) *Desire In Language: A Semiotic Approach to Literature and Art*,

Thomas Gora, Alice Jardine and Leon Roudiez (trans.), New York: Columbia University Press.

Lacan, Jacques (1992) *The Ethics of Psychoanalysis 1959–1960: The Seminar of Jacques Lacan Book 7*, Jacques-Alain Miller (ed.), Dennis Porter (trans.), London: Tavistock/Routledge.

—— (1988) *The Seminar of Jacques Lacan: Book 1 1953–1954*, Jacques-Alain Miller (ed.), John Forrester (trans.), New York and London: Norton.

—— (1988b) *The Seminar of Jacques Lacan: Book 2 1954–1955*, Jacques-Alain Miller (ed.), John Forrester (trans.), New York and London: Norton.

—— (1977) *Ecrits: A Selection*, Alan Sheridan (trans.), London: Tavistock.

—— (1977b) *The Four Fundamental Concepts of Psychoanalysis*, Alan Sheridan (trans.), Harmondsworth: Penguin.

—— (1973) 'Seminar on "The Purloined Letter"', *Yale French Studies*, 48.

Laplanche, Jean (1976) *Life and Death in Psychoanalysis*, Jeffrey Mehlman (trans.), Baltimore: Johns Hopkins University Press.

Laplanche, Jean and Pontalis, J.-B. (1986) 'Fantasy and the origins of sexuality', in *Formations of Fantasy*, Victor Burgin, James and Cora Kaplan (eds), London: Methuen.

—— (1973) *The Language of Psychoanalysis*, Donald Nicholson-Smith (trans.), London: Hogarth.

de Lauretis, Teresa (1987) *Technologies of Gender: Essays on Theory, Film, and Fiction*, London: Macmillan.

—— (1984) 'Desire in narrative', in *Alice Doesn't*, Bloomington: Indiana University Press.

Levinas, Emmanuel (1985) *Ethics and Infinity*, Pittsburgh: Duquesne University Press.

MacCabe, Colin (ed.) (1981) *The Talking Cure: Essays in Psychoanalysis and Language*, London: Macmillan.

Marcus, Steven (1984) *Freud and the Culture of Psychoanalysis*, Boston: Allen & Unwin.

Masson, Jeffrey Moussaieff (1985) (ed. and trans.) *The Complete Letters of Sigmund Freud to Wilhelm Fliess 1887–1904*, Cambridge, Mass.: Belknap/Harvard.

Melville, Stephen (1986) *Philosophy Beside Itself: On Deconstruction and Modernism*, Minneapolis: University of Minnesota Press.

Mitchell, Juliet (1974) *Psychoanalysis and Feminism*, Harmondsworth: Penguin.

Mitchell, Juliet and Rose, Jacqueline (1982) *Feminine Sexuality: Jacques Lacan and the Ecole Freudienne*, London: Macmillan.

Muller, John P. and Richardson, William J. (1982) *Lacan and Language: A Reader's Guide to Ecrits*, New York: International University Press.

Münchow, Michael and Samdashani, Sonu (1994) *Speculations after Freud: Psychoanalysis, Philosophy, Culture*, London: Routledge.

Pfeiffer, Ernst (1972) *Sigmund Freud and Lou Andreas-Salomé Letters*, New York: Norton.

Ragland-Sullivan, Ellie (1986) *Jacques Lacan and the Philosophy of Psychoanalysis*, Urbana: University of Illinois.

—— (1984) 'The magnetism between reader and text: prolegomena to a Lacanian poetics', *Poetics*, 13: 381–406.

Ricoeur, Paul (1978) *The Rule of Metaphor*, Robert Czerny (trans.), London: Routledge & Kegan Paul.

—— (1970) *Freud and Philosophy: An Essay in Interpretation*, David Savage (trans.), New Haven: Yale University Press.

Rorty, Richard (1989) *Contingency, Irony and Solidarity*, Cambridge: Cambridge University Press.

Rose, Jacqueline (1986) *Sexuality in the Field of Vision*, London: Verso.

Schneiderman, Stuart (1983) *Jacques Lacan: The Death of an Intellectual Hero*, Cambridge, Mass.: Harvard University Press.

Spivak, Gayatri (1989) 'Feminism and deconstruction again: negotiating with unacknowledged masculinism', in T. Brennan (1989) *Between Feminism and Psychoanalysis*.

—— (1980) 'Revolutions that as yet have no model: Derrida's Limited Inc', *Diacritics*, Winter: 29–49.

Strouse, Jean (1985) *Women and Analysis: Dialogues on Psychoanalytic Views of Femininity*, Boston: G.K. Hall.

Weber, Samuel (1991) *Return to Freud: Jacques Lacan's Dislocation of Psychoanalysis*, Michael Levine (trans.), Cambridge: Cambridge University Press.

—— (1982) *The Legend of Freud*, Minneapolis: University of Minnesota Press.

—— (1973) 'The sideshow: or remarks on a canny moment', *Modern Language Notes*, 88: 1102–34.

Wittgenstein, Ludwig (1979) *Wittgenstein's Lectures Cambridge, 1932–1935*, Alice Ambrose (ed.), Oxford: Basil Blackwell.

—— (1966) *Lectures and Conversations on Aesthetics, Psychology and Religious Belief*, Cyril Barrett (ed.), Berkeley: University of California Press.

Wollheim, Richard and Hopkins, James (eds) (1982) *Philosophical Essays on Freud*, Cambridge: Cambridge University Press.

Yale French Studies (1977) (1980) 55/56 'Literature and psychoanalysis: the question of reading otherwise'.

Zizek, Slavoj (1991) *Looking Awry: An Introduction to Jacques Lacan through Popular Culture*, Cambridge, Mass.: MIT Press.

Index